D0546078

G . F
SMITH
1885 ONWARDS

Editor's welcome

All eyes are on London as a centre of finance and global affairs. But the capital's popular allure comes from the strength of its creative industries. With tourists, students and young professionals pitching up in the millions to participate, the city has developed a spirited, multicultural creative clout. And it never stands still.

This guide focuses on the capital's thriving design scene: its boutiques, vintage dealers, design galleries and creative workshops. We've plucked out the destinations that best reflect that scene and reviewed them by neighbourhood, devising user-friendly maps to help navigate the city's sprawl.

Of course, behind every venue are talented individuals who implement their vision with gusto. In this edition, we've also interviewed personalities from Design Museum director Deyan Sudjic to veteran retailer Zeev Aram, from Marylebone trailblazers to East London mavericks. And we've gained access to private studios run by Barber Osgerby and Fredrikson Stallard. No other London guide boasts such widespread coverage or such entrée.

My advice is to tackle each area by foot, to savour the local flavour. Allow yourself to get lost and remember to look up – the city's peculiarities are often above head height. When you're running low on energy, enjoy a coffee, cocktail or meal at one of the restaurants or bars we recommend in each chapter. Even die-hard devotees of design will discover something new.

BRAUN

Contents

Area chapters

Features

Profiles & interviews

LONDON

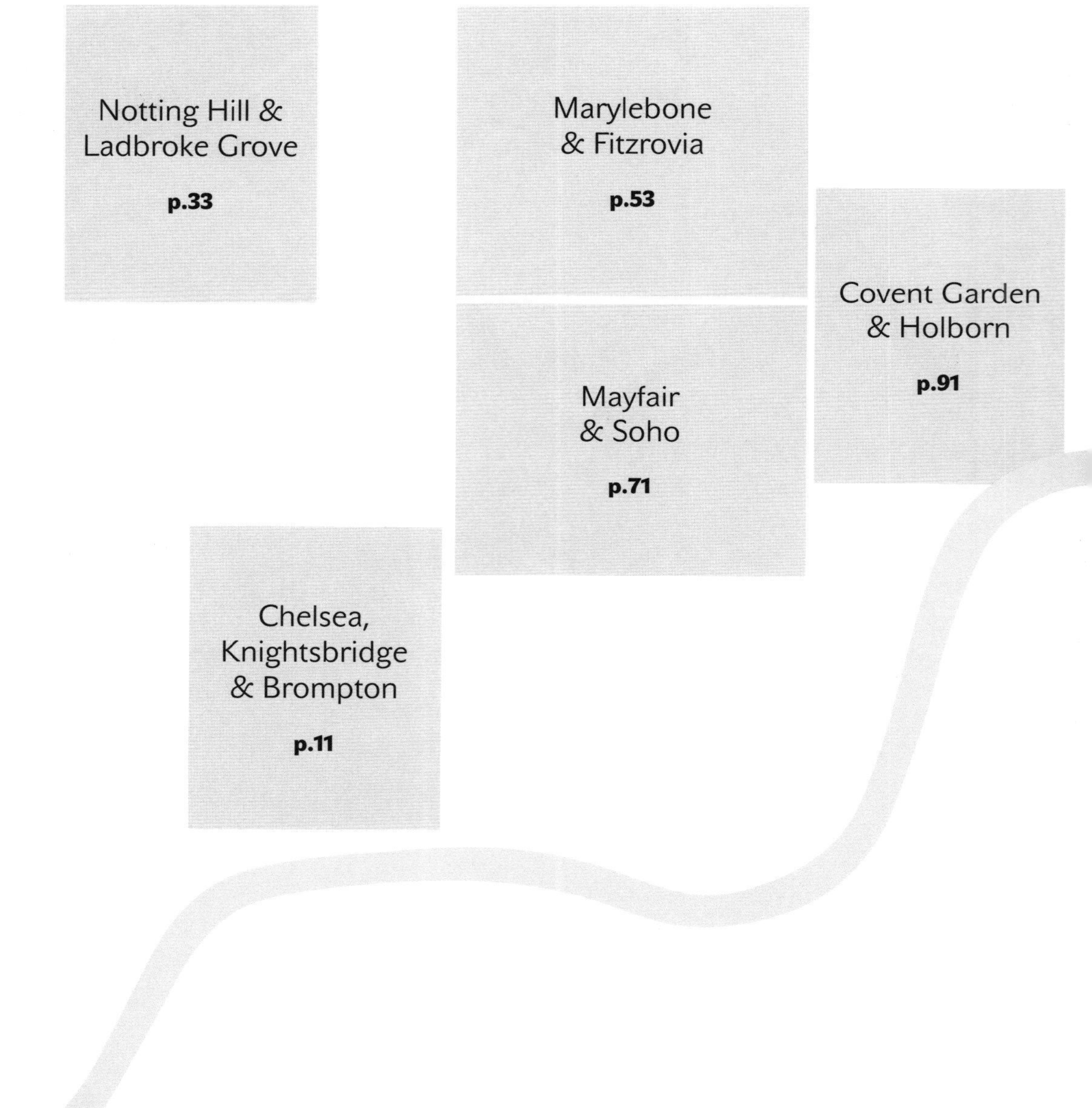

Notting Hill & Ladbroke Grove

p.33

Marylebone & Fitzrovia

p.53

Covent Garden & Holborn

p.91

Mayfair & Soho

p.71

Chelsea, Knightsbridge & Brompton

p.11

CHELSEA KNIGHTSBRIDGE & BROMPTON

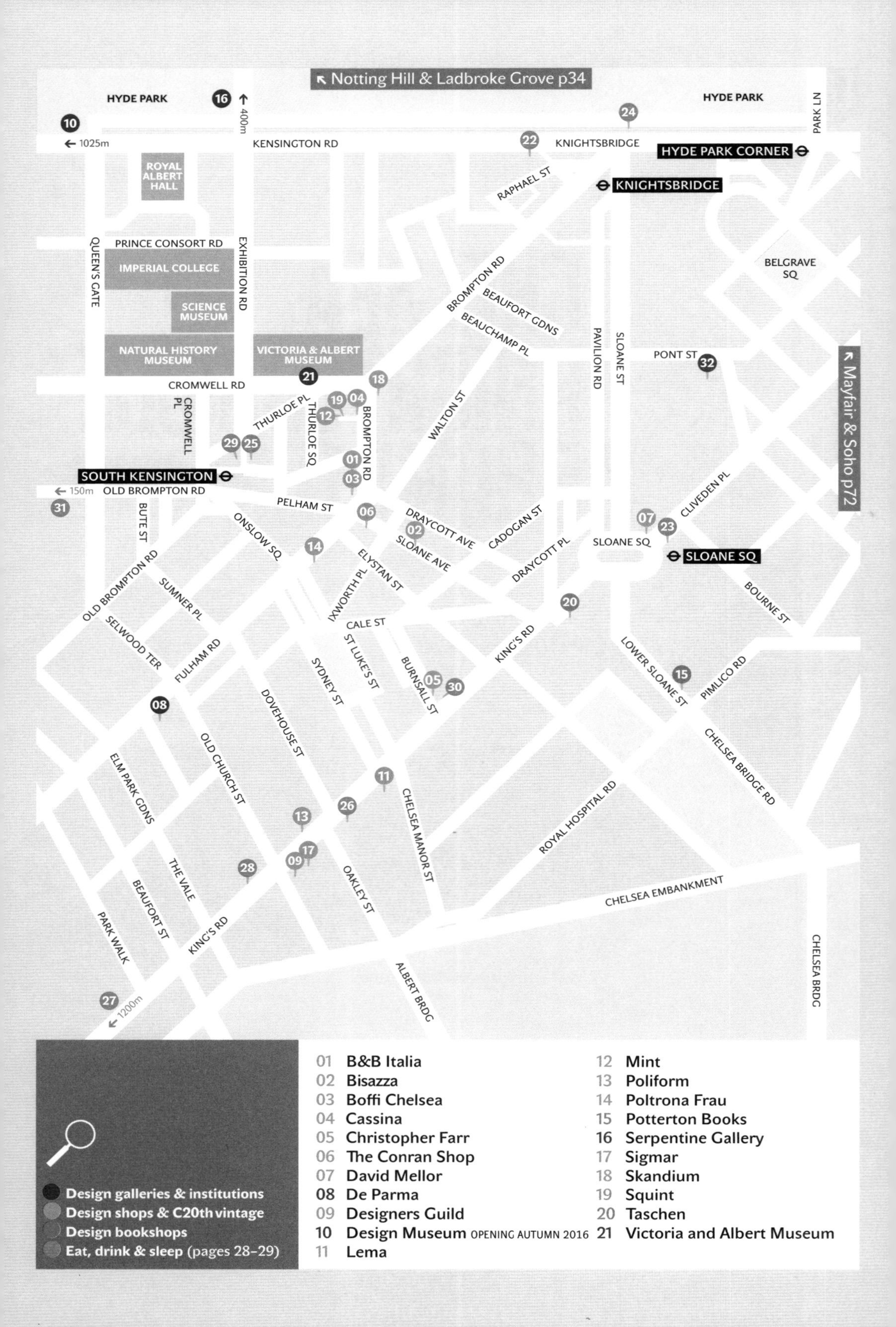

Notting Hill & Ladbroke Grove p34
HYDE PARK
HYDE PARK
PARK LN
400m
1025m
KENSINGTON RD
KNIGHTSBRIDGE
HYDE PARK CORNER
KNIGHTSBRIDGE
RAPHAEL ST
ROYAL ALBERT HALL
PRINCE CONSORT RD
QUEEN'S GATE
EXHIBITION RD
IMPERIAL COLLEGE
SCIENCE MUSEUM
NATURAL HISTORY MUSEUM
VICTORIA & ALBERT MUSEUM
BELGRAVE SQ
BROMPTON RD
BEAUFORT GDNS
BEAUCHAMP PL
PAVILION RD
SLOANE ST
PONT ST
Mayfair & Soho p72
CROMWELL RD
CROMWELL PL
THURLOE PL
THURLOE SQ
BROMPTON RD
WALTON ST
SOUTH KENSINGTON
150m
OLD BROMPTON RD
PELHAM ST
ONSLOW SQ
DRAYCOTT AVE
SLOANE AVE
CADOGAN ST
DRAYCOTT PL
SLOANE SQ
CLIVEDEN PL
SLOANE SQ
BUTE ST
OLD BROMPTON RD
SUMNER PL
ELYSTAN ST
IXWORTH PL
BOURNE ST
SELWOOD TER
CALE ST
KING'S RD
LOWER SLOANE ST
PIMLICO RD
FULHAM RD
ST LUKE'S ST
SYDNEY ST
BURNSALL ST
DOVEHOUSE ST
OLD CHURCH ST
ELM PARK GDNS
CHELSEA BRIDGE RD
CHELSEA MANOR ST
ROYAL HOSPITAL RD
THE VALE
OAKLEY ST
CHELSEA EMBANKMENT
BEAUFORT ST
KING'S RD
PARK WALK
1200m
ALBERT BRDG
CHELSEA BRDG
Design galleries & institutions
Design shops & C20th vintage
Design bookshops
Eat, drink & sleep (pages 28–29)
01 B&B Italia
02 Bisazza
03 Boffi Chelsea
04 Cassina
05 Christopher Farr
06 The Conran Shop
07 David Mellor
08 De Parma
09 Designers Guild
10 Design Museum OPENING AUTUMN 2016
11 Lema
12 Mint
13 Poliform
14 Poltrona Frau
15 Potterton Books
16 Serpentine Gallery
17 Sigmar
18 Skandium
19 Squint
20 Taschen
21 Victoria and Albert Museum

Chelsea, Knightsbridge & Brompton

The rebranding of the Sloane's stomping ground as Brompton Quarter continues apace, as purveyors of chintz and Chippendale make way for European flagships and highly specialised contemporary craft. The crisp, clean innovative design makes an alluring counterpoint to the splendid red-brick Victorian architecture, dating back to the Great Exhibition of 1851. As museums like the V&A get stronger and more relevant each year, they're balanced by commercial newcomers like Lema, the Italian family company art-directed by Piero Lissoni.

01 **B&B Italia**
250 Brompton Road SW3 2AS
020 7591 8111
bebitalia.it
Mon-Sat 10-6, Sun 12-5

A giant of Italian modernism, B&B designs furniture staples that are elegantly refined yet unshowy, ample yet unimposing, vibrant yet subtle. Its cavernous, glass-fronted flagship, a former car showroom converted by architect John Pawson and designed by Antonio Citterio, is not just a store, it's an experience.

02 **Bisazza**
60 Sloane Avenue SW3 3DD
020 7584 8837
bisazza.com
Mon-Fri 10-6

A browse around Bisazza's Chelsea headquarters is exceptionally pleasurable. The company has always been about drama, and here it shows off its iridescent mosaics to Renaissance-grade effect. The artful scenes are a perfect complement to the Marcel Wanders and Nendo bathroom lines, available here. If you have a space like this Sloane Avenue jewel, all the better.

03 **Boffi Chelsea**
254 Brompton Road SW3 2AS
020 7590 8910
boffiuk.com
Mon-Sat 10-6

Like its neighbour B&B Italia, the showroom of highly functional kitchen and bathroom specialist Boffi goes on for miles but is an entirely different experience: intense, dramatic and accessorised not with dividing screens but walls of bamboo. These soften the severe lines of the product and give the rooms more of a lounge feel, enhanced by some warmer materials like textured tiling and seagrass walls. A Boffi space is a space to be lived in, no matter what the ultimate purpose.

Treasure hunter
Lina Kanafani, *Mint*

Layered in textural fabrics, adorned in jewellery fashioned from stacked-paper beads, Lina Kanafani embodies her dedication to rigorous experimental design. And yet, as a recent expat from Jordan, she studied to be a nutritionist. London would have been a rather different place had Kanafani not gone rogue and opened Mint in a Marylebone storefront in 1998. Her singular approach and dedication to 'different' distinguished her during the big-brand invasion that ensued. And today, Mint is not just a place to bask in polished design, but a primer in fine, handcrafted art.

When you moved to this location from Marylebone six years ago, did you experience a shift in philosophy or perspective?
I always liked this location, although it was not the right position for footfall. So once we moved in, our old way – being about small things, ceramics and so on – didn't work. We needed to become more like a gallery, more upmarket, on a much bigger scale. Our clients now are mostly interior designers. There are about 1,000 interior designers in this area – it's shocking. Now we have to buy things that complement what is surrounding us in the neighbourhood, at Christian Liaigre, B&B Italia, and Cassina.

Are you still commissioning new work from designers?
With some pieces, I just ask designers to make changes to scale and materials, to go with what I envisage will please our customers. With a table, I'll work out the proportions in a way the interior designers will understand, but the mechanism will stay the same.

04 Cassina
242 Brompton Road SW3 2BB
020 7584 0000
cassina.com
Mon-Sat 10-6.30, Thurs 10-7, Sun 12-6

At nearly 90 years old, the Cassina brand has had its share of contributors, and this strategically lit showroom, designed with steely aplomb by Piero Lissoni, reflects that. In one corner you might find a pair of Hill House chairs by Charles Rennie Mackintosh (an unlikely collaborator among the Corbusiers and Perriands) enhanced by a vertical arrangement of gilt mirrors. And in another, a newly designed Patrick Norguet P22 wing chair next to a Cicognino side table by Franco Albini.

05 Christopher Farr
6 Burnsall Street SW3 3ST
020 7349 0888
christopherfarr.com
Mon-Fri 10-6

Established in 1988, Slade-trained painter Christopher Farr was a pioneer in commissioning big-name creatives to turn their attention to the floor, and he has worked with the likes of Andrée Putman, Kate Blee and Romeo Gigli on limited-edition designs. True to his artist origins, Farr's showroom off the King's Road is more like an atelier, encompassing his studio, stockroom and collection of samples in the same barn-like space.

06 The Conran Shop
Michelin House, 81 Fulham Road
SW3 6RD
020 7589 7401
conranshop.co.uk
Mon-Fri 10-6, Wed-Thurs 10-7,
Sat 10-6.30, Sun 12-6

Just when you think you might be tiring of the whole Conran ethos, its spaces get a new attitude and lease of life, thanks in part to creative director Jasper Conran, whose influence has brought about a decluttering, a fresh lick of white paint and a look that is decidedly more fun. Conran's own-designed furniture gets good play here but also features well alongside favourites by Bertoia, Benchmark and the Bouroullecs.

07 David Mellor
4 Sloane Square SW1W 8EE
020 7730 4259
davidmellordesign.com
Mon–Sat 9.30–6, Sun 11–5

This tableware retailer stocks the full range of Sheffield-born designer David Mellor's handcrafted cutlery, as well as a stable of brands and designers, among them iittala, Richard Batterham, and Sarah Petherick, who makes a range of objects from Vietnamese water buffalo horn. Now run by Mellor's son Corin, the store has a lower level that trumps the ground floor space in size and scope. This is where you'll find small appliances, pottery, gardening tools, and even extra virgin olive oil.

08 De Parma
247 Fulham Road SW3 6HY
020 7352 2414
deparma.com
Mon–Sat 10–6

De Parma's collectible midcentury design skews older than a lot of the modernism so long in vogue in the eastern reaches of the city. Gary De Sparham's curated collection focuses on the 1940s and 1950s, and he has an obvious fascination with the Italian heavies of the era: there is always something in store representing Ico Parisi, Gio Ponti or Piero Fornasetti. Added excitement comes in through accessories like lamps by Stilnovo and Gino Sarfatti.

09 Designers Guild
267–277 King's Road SW3 5EN
020 7351 5775
designersguild.com
Mon–Sat 10–6, Sun 12–5

This showroom is the product of Tricia Guild's successful formula of unusual midcentury design plus eccentric artwork plus

I work a lot with Maarten Baas; with Andrea Forti and Eleonora Dal Farra of Alcarol; with Andere Monjo, who did our Rain tables in steel and distressed mirrors – we can do that one table in endless mutations. We've also worked with Pia [Wüstenberg] ever since she was an RCA graduate. Her experimental glass is in all the museums now.

The retail landscape has changed since you launched Mint. How do you stay relevant?
By doing a lot of hard work. We have two main shows a year, where everything is totally new. And designers are bringing things in on a weekly basis. I now do interior consultation, so I can afford to throw parties, go to shows and encourage new designers. Showing big names doesn't work for us because there are too many around here already. I can't compete with Moroso.

Most of the things we sell now are related to craft. I'm more inclined to show pieces like the Tree Light, where the recycled birch takes six months to dry. Or the console made from wood recycled from abandoned houses near Bologna. One table is made with wood poles from the Venice lagoon, hundreds of years old and eaten by molluscs. I'm looking at new concepts, new materials, new ways of thinking, because everything has been done. The way we combine it here makes it more eclectic, more desirable.

Where do you search for new talent?
The Salone del Mobile in Milan has always been the top show. But I go to a lot of graduate shows – the show at the Royal College of Art, at Design Academy Eindhoven, in Prague and Berlin. The only show I don't go to is New York.

Can you describe the Mint style in a few words?
It's elegant, it's rich, the materials look expensive. It's finely tuned and luxurious, but it's playful.

Does that translate to expensive?
I'm not expensive compared to places like Carpenters Workshop Gallery or David Gill. I'm more like [Spazio] Rossana Orlandi in Milan. But I try to be more tidy than her. EH

12 Mint 2 North Terrace SW3 2BA (See page 20)

one-off accessories, all adhering to the highly saturated palette continuously refreshed by the designer. This takes some of the pressure off the textiles and allows them to be showcased imaginatively on soft furnishings by Fritz Hansen and Moroso.

10 Design Museum
224–238 Kensington High Street
W8 6AG
020 7403 6933
designmuseum.org

Architect John Pawson is redesigning the former Commonwealth Institute to become a new home for the Design Museum, currently based at Shad Thames. It should be completed in autumn 2016, but until then, the 25-year-old institution founded by Terence Conran will remain in situ with its 2015 designers-in-residence Alexa Pollmann, Hefin Jones, Chris Green and Stephanie Hornig. Its final exhibition, Cycle Revolution, explores the bicycle designs that have changed commuting in London and beyond immeasurably. Make a detour off the Thames Path for tea in the café and a mooch around one of the finest museum shops in town. (See pages 18–23 and page 181)

11 Lema
183 King's Road SW3 5EB
020 3761 3299
lema-uk.com
Mon–Sat 10–6

Occupying two floors in a beautiful building on King's Road, Lema's showroom is the very embodiment of slick Italian design, designed by its art director Piero Lissoni (see page 25). Lema is one of the leading producers of custom-built shelving systems and wardrobes, and here you can specify your requirements with expert assistance, as well as browse its growing collections of furniture from its Home Collection designed by the likes of Christophe Pillet, Roberto Lazzeroni, and Ludovica and Roberto Palomba among others.

London's **Design Museum** has occupied a defunct banana warehouse in Shad Thames since 1989. But in 2016 it will move into the former Commonwealth Institute on Kensington High Street, the interior overhauled by minimalist architect John Pawson. **Deyan Sudjic**, author, critic and the museum's director since 2006, has raised £45 million to make the move possible. We talk to him about the relocation to West London

12 Mint
2 North Terrace SW3 2BA
020 7225 2228
mintshop.co.uk
Mon-Sat 10.30-6.30, Thurs 10.30-7.30

Lina Kanafani is the sage on the mountain of design retailers, blessed with a special sense for what will catch the fancy of her clientele. She stocks incomparable works of functional art, much from young unknowns, that must be a thrill to curate. What first catches your eye are the vessels, potted pieces that meld ancient techniques with contemporary finishes, and the unusual wood and blown-glass vessel-shaped artworks by London-based Pia Wüstenberg. Then it's the rich collection of resin-embedded wood tables and lighting shrouded in mottled glass. Kanafani layers them with the expertise of a Hollywood set designer – it's hardly surprising that she operates an interior-design consultation from the premises. (See pages 14–17)

13 Poliform
278 King's Road SW3 5AW
020 7368 7600
poliformuk.com
Mon-Sat 10-6

Poliform is a little more slick and sterile than its Italian peers in the area, with spare, geometric tables, expansive beds and wardrobe systems styled with the minimum of accoutrements. However, with over 40 years in business and more than a decade in its cubist Paolo Piva-designed London flagship, which has recently undergone fresh renovations and expanded in size, it shows no signs of flailing. Highlights include Jean-Marie Massaud's Ventura Lounge and Paola Navone's Bug armchair, as well as the high spec Varenna kitchens, fitted with slick Gaggenau appliances. Everything on display acts as a muted backdrop on which you can layer your own personality at home. Should you require some guidance, the on-site design service should be most helpful.

You've been with the Design Museum for nearly 10 years now and have seen it through some huge changes. What was the state of it when you joined?
I was appointed at a moment when it had already gone through a transition – [previous director] Alice Rawsthorn was a shot of energy in the arm for the museum. She managed to change the general sense of design being only about chairs and brought it alive. But the museum was almost domestic in scale – a staff of 40 with a restricted budget living hand to mouth. We decided it was time to invest in the future and grow. We went from 106,000 to 200,000 visitors annually and grew our staff to 70. I say we've grown up without growing old.

Your tenure has seen London mature as a design centre. Is design more seriously considered as an art form now?
In some ways, art is what really has happened – the eruption of the art scene in London. In the 1970s, the only way artists could survive in London was by teaching

Previous page, the original Commonwealth Institute roof

Above, how the entrance foyer for the new Design Museum will look

part time, and that's changed enormously. What makes London stand out are its colleges and universities, which attract bright people around the world. They've cemented London's reputation as a place where great things happen. I'm concerned that's being eroded now. Education has been somewhat industrialised and turned into too business-like a process.

What are the most marked changes in London as you've seen them in the past decade?
Just looking out the window from the museum, I see an eruption of high-rises. My view of Tower Bridge is now compromised by the unattractive, lumpen Walkie-Talkie. The Leadenhall Building has risen, Renzo Piano's tower has made its mark on the horizon. We've taught ourselves to believe London is a conservative place where change is resisted, but it's actually closer to Shanghai or Singapore. In design terms, it's managed to develop a critical mass of studios that work

PCH

worldwide and allow a conversation to take place about the subject. London is a big enough city that various approaches to design can coexist. You've got the school of Ron Arad; younger, gifted designers like Martino Gamper and Paul Cocksedge; and the technocrats who went off to California to work with Jonathan Ive. The range as well as the depth of talent makes London important.

Have any designs emerged in your time at the museum that you'd consider future classics?
That's a complicated thing because time can be cruel to design. At the moment we're seeing the process of change speeding up faster and the sense in which design is no longer entirely based on the physical object. One of the things we started doing when I got to the Design Museum is the Designs of the Year, where we exhibit 100 projects from around the world. In 2008 the winner was Yves Béhar's One Laptop per Child – while it was formally interesting and worthwhile, the idea of a low-cost tablet now seems very dated. In 2009 it was Shepard Fairey's poster for Obama, and things tarnished there quickly. Later it was Gov.uk, a website that allowed the British state to communicate clearly with its citizens – a classic, but it'll probably be gone in a few years. What does a classic mean in this period?

The architect John Pawson has taken on the design of the new building. Why do you think that he was right for the job?
We selected John because his work is refined but restrained, and with a building such as the Commonwealth Institute, which is already flamboyant, we needed an architect whose voice would be restrained. Also, he'd not done a public building in London, and it was interesting to make that possible.

Do you think that your move from east to west will alter your perspective?
The scale will shift. We'll go from 3,000 square metres to 10,000, with three times the exhibition space and half a million visitors a year. We're looking to talk beyond the converted and engage with a wider group.

Your obvious legacy at the museum will be this building, but what else?
I hope it's what's in the building more than anything else. The museum can't be my voice. It can't be one individual's voice. It's a platform. EH

"With a building such as the Commonwealth Institute, which is already flamboyant, we needed an architect whose voice would be restrained."

10 Design Museum 224–238 Kensington High Street W8 6AG (See pages 17 and 181)

Opposite, the Design Museum is set to move into its new home in 2016

183

Dream house
Piero Lissoni, *Lema*

Only design-philes will understand the impact of the great Milanese minimalist Piero Lissoni on Chelsea, one of London's most august neighbourhoods. Since the 1980s, Lissoni has been known for product design and architecture commissioned by companies like Alessi, Kartell, Boffi and Cassina. The latter he helped establish in Chelsea with two very different Brompton Road boutiques. Recently he added a third with the 400-square-metre flagship for Lema, a family-run company established in 1970. The King's Road townhouse is laid out like a family home devoted to Lema furnishings by the likes of Raw-Edges, Nendo, Neri & Hu and, of course, Lissoni himself. We met him after the grand opening.

What brought you and Lema to London?
After 20 years with Lema, we started to discuss doing something more international for the company, to be in a special place abroad. And a special place, for me, is London. The idea was to open a shop that looks like a house, with a huge window onto the street. Inside, it's a cross between a townhouse and a loft.

You've designed three boutiques in Chelsea – for Boffi, Cassina and now Lema. Why Chelsea?
It's an interesting quarter, where you can walk and find cafes, restaurants, nice antique shops, furniture shops and fashion – but not the usual labels. Everything's sophisticated to the eye, in very good taste. And Chelsea Market is like a sophisticated courtyard.

Was it a challenge to fit your minimalist aesthetic into this Victorian envelope?
It's not enough to be just modern, contemporary or minimalist – you have to accept the special integration with the historic building. Good taste is about combining different codes – to be modernist but also contaminated by history.

14 Poltrona Frau
147–153 Fulham Road SW3 6SN
020 7589 3846
poltronafrau.com
Mon–Sat 10–6, Sun 12–6

Established in 1912, Poltrona Frau is considered the jewel in the crown of the Poltrona Frau Group (see page 114). Famous for high quality leather furniture, the brand launched this flagship in the autumn of 2015 to show off its traditional Italian craftsmanship amid Chelsea's wealth belt. Spread across two floors, the open plan space brings together room sets of smart dining chairs and seductive sofas, not forgetting the iconic 1919 rococo armchair by Renzo Frau himself.

15 Potterton Books
93 Lower Sloane Street SW1W 8DA
020 7730 4235
pottertonbookslondon.com
Mon–Sat 10–6

Where you might physically wander through other bookshops, here you can't do much more than shuffle to the opposite stacks. The content is worth a go, though, because the speciality here is 'inspiration'. Printing, fashion, photography, crafts, garden design, architecture… it's all here, sometimes in rare form, often signed by local authors.

16 Serpentine Gallery
Kensington Gardens W2 3XA
020 7402 6075
serpentinegallery.org
Daily 10–6

The Serpentine is known for securing a roll call of esteemed ground-breakers, from Thomas Demand and Bridget Riley to Yoko Ono and Rosemarie Trockel. It now has a second space across the eponymous river, a renovated 200-year-old Palladian building, with a café annex designed by Zaha Hadid. But it is probably best known for its highly anticipated annual summer pavilions by legends such as Frank Gehry, Jean Nouvel, and Herzog & de Meuron with Ai Weiwei.

And what elements of the Lema interior are you most proud of?
The stairs. I'm so glad they are in there. But also it's an old shop that is quite elegant yet at the same time a little shabby – in an English way. Especially the ceiling. We've respected what has happened over the years to the ceiling.

What would you say are your favourite cities to design in?
I like Berlin, Hong Kong, Tokyo, Milan and Paris. But London is one of my favourites, for the vitality, for the quality, for the traffic, for the museums and energy.

Are there any London-based designers that you watch closely?
Jasper Morrison – he is kind of aristocratic but at the same time he's also a rebel, and his work is super-current. Another one for his currency is the architect John Pawson. When you see something of his, you immediately feel the complexity, the intellectual point of view. It's not enough to make something clean – you have to put a lot of thought into it. The form of simplicity is the public face of complexity. You have to work around a lot of details to minimalise everything. So both of them are, I think, the most important designers in Britain. **EH**

11 **Lema** 183 King's Road SW3 5ED (See page 17)

Previous page, the exterior of Lema's King's Road store

Below, the store is laid out like a family home with Lema furnishings

17 Sigmar
263 King's Road SW3 5EL
020 7751 5801
sigmarlondon.com
Mon-Fri 10-6

Sigmar's enchanting treasures are mostly from Northern Europe's golden years (1940s–1960s), as well as a few treats from today. Run by Ebba Thott and Nina Hertig, interiors experts with extraordinary enthusiasm, it packs more into the first square metre than many shops carry across the floor – you'll find pieces by Carl Auböck, Ilmari Tapiovaara and Pierre Forsell. Quality prevails across everything, ideal for those hunting for design that lasts.

18 Skandium
245–249 Brompton Road
SW3 2EP
020 7584 2066
skandium.com
Mon-Sat 10-6.30, Thurs 10-7, Sun 11-5

Within this sizeable corner space, Skandium customers can browse a carefully curated display of Scandinavian classics, new innovations and a smattering of kitsch, together with complementary pieces from other European brands. Owners Magnus Englund and Chrystina Schmidt import only what they love – continually introducing offerings that distinguish them from the now ubiquitous Scandi purveyors found elsewhere.

19 Squint
1 North Terrace SW3 2BA
020 7589 6839
squintlimited.com
Mon-Sat 10-6, Thurs 10-7, Sun 12- 5

Squint HQ takes the popular patchwork motif to the max, and perhaps overboard, to the point where you can't see much else but squares of Skittles-hued velvet. But there are alternatives in the mix, if equally colourful, including hand-embroidered Thai cushions and chandeliers, styled with traditional French flourishes yet wrapped in jewel-toned velvet.

20 Taschen
12 Duke of York Square SW3 4LY
020 7881 0795
taschen.com
Mon-Fri 10-6, Wed, Sat 10-7, Sun 12-6

High-end German art book publisher Taschen did well to hire Philippe Starck to outfit its Chelsea store. Two snug spaces are stacked one upon the other, building a series of immense storage islands down the middle to serve as browsing stations for its monographs and tomes, which cover everything from film and fetishism to painting and pornography.

21 Victoria and Albert Museum
Cromwell Road SW7 2RL
020 7907 7073
vam.ac.uk
Daily 10- 5.45, Friday 10-10

Devoted to contemporary design and architecture, the V&A often pays homage to the modern greats, but its collection spans 2,000 years of design on all continents. The building is a suitable venue. Its regal spaces are ample enough that even the most monolithic marbles – and attendant mobs – can breathe. Special temporary exhibitions are centrally located, along with the Fashion and Sculpture galleries, and legions of Asian tapestries. Recharge in the cafe or the John Madejski Garden, which is a blessed retreat in summer.

For opulent cocktails
22 Il Bar
Bulgari Hotel
171 Knightsbridge SW7 1DW
020 7151 1010
bulgarihotels.com

With its highly polished black granite floor, hammered circular silver bar and titanium ceiling, Il Bar oozes overstated elegance. It is also a very impressive place to try quintessential British or Italian-inspired cocktails, such as a Mistaken Identity or a Morning Fog.

For tea and people watching
23 Colbert
50–53 Sloane Square SW1W 8AX
020 7730 2804
colbertchelsea.com

Sporting a classic French bistro-style interior with blood leather booths and chequered floors, this is a useful spot for some post-shopping tea or a pick-me-up – plus there are ample opportunities to watch the Chelsea set strut by.

For a historical dinner
24 Dinner by Heston Blumenthal
Mandarin Oriental,
66 Knightsbridge SW1X 7LA
020 7201 3833
mandarinoriental.com

The three Michelin-starred Fat Duck chef serves up food inspired by 14–19th century feasting menus.

For punchy morning coffee
25 Fernandez & Wells
8a Exhibition Road SW7 2HF
020 7589 7473
fernandezandwells.com

A sleek operation from the people known for their Soho coffee and jamon bars.

For elegant breakfast
26 The Ivy Chelsea Garden
197 King's Road SW3 5EQ
020 3301 0300
theivychelseagarden.com

The elegant sister of the original Ivy restaurant. Try truffled eggs while admiring its botanical beauty – sage green and burnt orange furnishings and a splendid garden.

For fiery drinks and snacks
27 Koji
58 New King's Road SW6 4LS
020 7731 2520
koji.restaurant

This flashy bar, spruced up with feathery lights, sends out chilli lemongrass martinis, while a quietly brilliant Nobu-trained chef creates Asian and South American combinations like ceviche or yuzu sweetcorn.

For zippy lunch
28 Kurobuta
312 King's Road SW3 5UH
020 3475 4158
kurobuta-london.com

Low-key service, an open kitchen and top notch cooking are the main elements at Scott Hallsworth's modern Japanese restaurant, formerly a pop-up.

For sweet treats
29 Patisserie des Reves
13 Exhibition Road SW7 2HE
020 3603 8233
lapatisseriedesreves.com

This Parisian-style patisserie, with pretty pink and lime green walls, serves exquisite cakes, displayed under glass domes.

For hearty sharing food
30 Rabbit
172 King's Road SW3 4UP
020 3750 0172
rabbit-restaurant.com

A thoroughly British restaurant run by two brothers. Expect tractors on the ceiling and plates of off-trend cuts of meat.

For fishy lunch
31 Yashin Ocean House
117–119 Old Brompton Road
SW7 3RN
020 7373 3990
yashinocean.com

The interior blends Edwardian tiling with chequered flooring and an impressive bar at which chefs create plates of beautiful head-to-tail sushi, featuring fish skin and cod cheeks.

BOOK A ROOM

For luxury Brooklyn vibe
32 Belgraves
20 Chesham Place SW1X 8HQ
020 7858 0100
thompsonhotels.com/hotels/belgraves-london

Eat, drink & sleep

Above, overstated elegance reigns at the Bulgari Hotel's polished Il Bar

Below, Edwardian tiling and head-to-tail dining at Yashin Ocean House

Start me up

London's young designers are eschewing job security for a burgeoning be-your-own-boss culture – and changing the city's fabric in the process

London-based designer and one-man-brand Tom Dixon (see page 43) believes that, while business skills and creativity are essential for the modern day entrepreneur, these qualities are now within reach of everyone. The world is a very different place today, he says, compared to when he was embarking on his career in the early 1980s, untrained and welding furniture from scrap metal. Perhaps he paved the way, because now, he says: "Anyone can be a designer." More than that, he adds: "Anyone can be a manufacturer. And anyone can have immediate access to international markets."

A quick tour around Dixon's home city and it would appear that there are tens of thousands of people who seem to agree. London today is the city of the start-up, the culturepreneur and the kickstarter. And the most verdant and flourishing field to start up in? Design.

London, it would seem, is the city where individuals have the best chances to pitch their skills to the world. Potential collaborators are close at hand, and workspace is abundant, with endless options for mobile workers and collaboratives, a plethora of hubs and clubs and co-working ventures or, if you can afford it, a wide range of attractive and/or architecturally interesting self-contained options to choose from. As an economic powerhouse and international crossroads, many of the biggest brands in the world have chosen to make London their HQ – internationally, the city's brand stands for money (the costs may be high but so too are the rewards) and for colour (where diversity fuels creativity and connectivity like nowhere else). Ludicrous living costs aside, here everything a small business or entrepreneur needs is easily, instantly accessible. What's more, if you have a plan to escape the nine-to-five, there are plenty of inspiring examples in the city to offer living proof that it's possible, and encourage you to jump.

Blame a new generation disillusioned with the corporation, or accredit it to the new creative economy, but according to the Coworking Market Report Forecast, 40 per cent of the workforce will be freelancers, temps, independent contractors and solopreneurs by 2020. It's growing fast but it's also set to grow up: 70 per cent of those who currently fit in that innovative shared-workspace box are still under 40. In East London, coworking spaces are starting to outnumber hipster cafés – or, at least, the lines between the two are ever more blurry. The Trampery Old Street favours product start-ups over service companies and partners with Publicis, the advertising giant who has also conveniently opened Drugstore, which aims to hook up the resident companies with clients. Round the corner is Google Campus, a key player on the tech start-up scene in London, and just up the road in London Fields you'll find The Laundry – a huge industrial space with studios and a performance venue, attracting musicians, filmmakers and producers in droves.

At the start of 2015, Rohan Silva, the 33-year-old ex-advisor to David Cameron, co-founded a 'utopian' new collaborative off Brick Lane with Sam Aldenton (previous achievements include Feast and Dalston Roof Park). After spending £3million transforming an old carpet factory into 2,230 square metres of shared workspace, they opened Second Home to huge publicity and hype and there's a waiting list for desks – which are only allocated pending the owners' approval. "London is unique. There's no other city in the world that has the centre of national government, is the global capital of capital, has the leading tech hub on its continent, and is also home to some of the best media, advertising, retail, fashion and design talent in the world," says Silva.

The start-up community is exactly that – Second Home's members' club approach is a clever and fitting solution to filter the masses of aspiring self-employed. In East London districts like Shoreditch and Hackney, 'proper jobs' seem almost outdated. "There are many, many more small businesses than there were in the 1980s, but our cities and our buildings haven't evolved to keep pace with that," Silva told the *Evening Standard* after the launch. "Hopefully, Second Home is the first sort of salvo in what the workplaces of the future will look like." The pair are working on developing further sites in London and hope to expand the concept around the world.

"40 per cent of the workforce will be freelancers, temps, independent contractors and solopreneurs by 2020"

And while there are now more than five million SMEs in London, compared with 700,000 in 1980, the nature of these companies has also changed fundamentally: today's entrepreneurs are as much makers as they are doers. Collaborating with other talented individuals to fill the gaps they need as they go along, it's a fractal business model that keeps overheads low and creativity high.

The current generation of designers have the confidence and the means to design, produce and sell from the moment they graduate from one of London's top art colleges, but if there is any threat to London's position as the creative capital of the world, it's the rising cost of living. London is now the world's most expensive city in which to live and work, according to estate agent Savills, with the cost having risen almost 40 per cent since 2008. For many people, London prices are a major struggle. While it's certainly a concern, any creative exodus is still balanced by the irrefutable draw of the capital. Feeling the squeeze most are young couples, who want family-sized homes near good schools and are finding it impossible. Measures to attract millennials have no sway with this group of creative entrepreneurs in their mid- to late-30s and a vital pool of talent is flooding out of the city.

But money shortages don't always have to be a big problem. London has overtaken New York City and San Francisco to become the world capital of crowdfunding. With around 12 new crowdfunding projects launching from London each day, there's an average fully-funded success rate of 32 per cent.

Chancellor of the Exchequer George Osborne believes we are entering "a new era of innovative finance." The technologies being developed today, he says, will revolutionise the way we bank, the way we invest, the way companies raise money. "It will lead to new products, new services, new lenders."

Britain is home to around 80 different crowdfunding platforms, but the two biggest players are Crowdcube and Seedrs. "[The UK] is the best jurisdiction for crowdfunding in the world," says Jeff Lynn, the American-born founder of Seedrs. "The US and the rest of Europe are far behind the UK, which has a sensible regime that protects investors while still creating a commercial model in which to operate. Hats off to the government for their enthusiasm."

There were 1,604 projects in total that were launched across the UK through US site Kickstarter between January and March alone in 2015, attracting £6.3million in pledges. Another US site, Indiegogo, revealed a surge in activity for London-based start-ups, revealing a 700 per cent rise in UK start-up projects through its platform over the last year. Sidekick Creatives, a site specifically tailored to design, has contributed to the successful funding of a variety of projects in technology, fashion, publishing, furniture and product, and was nominated for a Design Museum Design of the Year award in 2014.

It's a simple equation: London plus the internet plus a little creative talent, multiplied by an open mind, access to cash and a lot of vision, equals one very exciting thing: a brave new world for designers, where anyone can potentially be anything they dream of.

Henrietta Thompson is editorial director of *Naked On The Piano*, design columnist at the *Telegraph*, and editor-at-large at *Wallpaper**

NOTTING HILL & LADBROKE GROVE

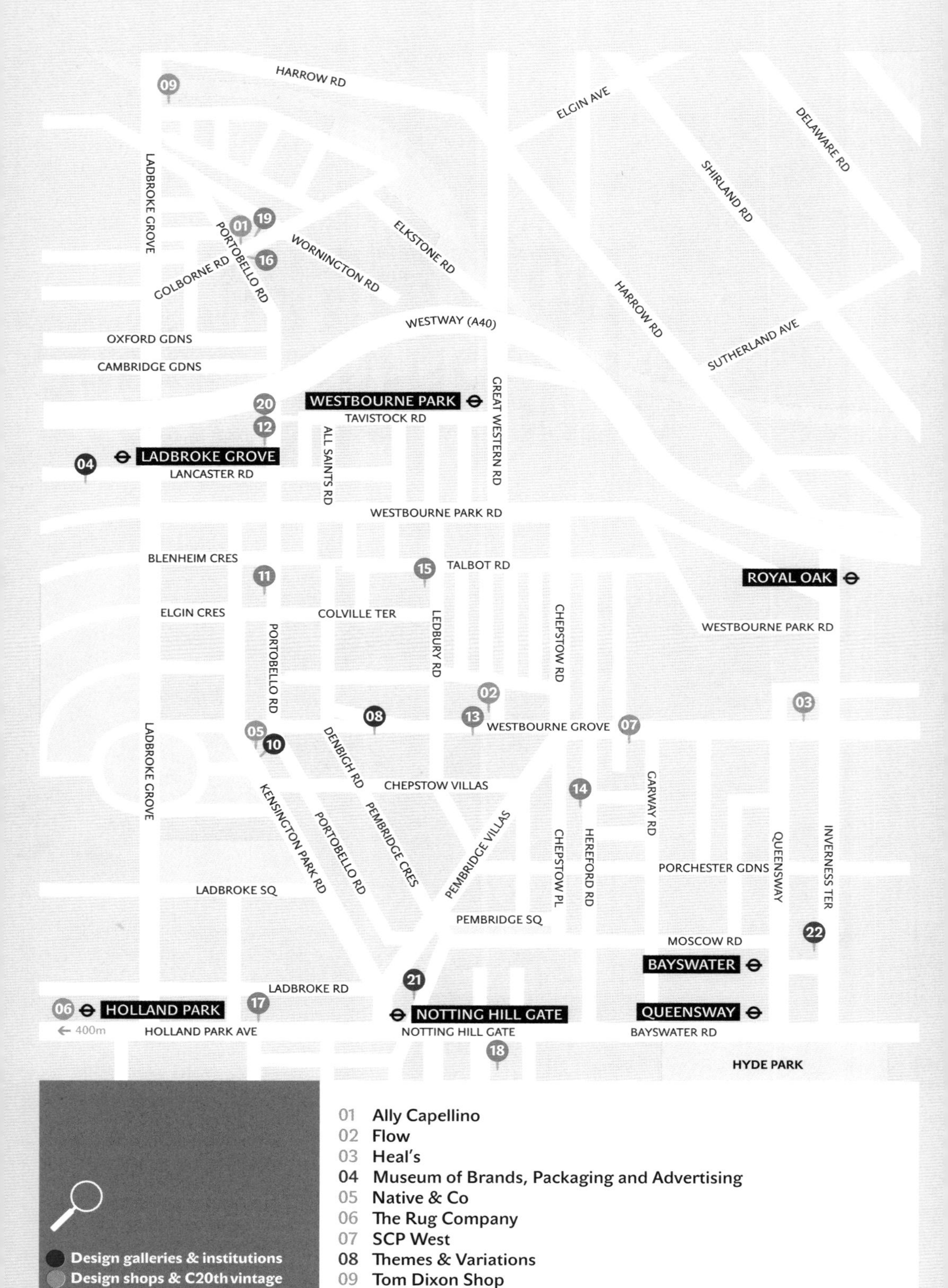

Design galleries & institutions
Design shops & C20th vintage
Design bookshops
Eat, drink & sleep (pages 46–47)

01 Ally Capellino
02 Flow
03 Heal's
04 Museum of Brands, Packaging and Advertising
05 Native & Co
06 The Rug Company
07 SCP West
08 Themes & Variations
09 Tom Dixon Shop
10 Vessel Gallery

Notting Hill & Ladbroke Grove

Considering the number of entrepreneurial designers living locally, it is perhaps no surprise that Notting Hill has evolved from a bohemian fashion destination into a design haven. Suzanne and Christopher Sharp run The Rug Company moments from their home; Tom Dixon has been here since childhood; Ross Lovegrove lives and works nearby; Sheridan Coakley of SCP is a former resident; and Yvonna Demczynska shares her living space with her craft gallery Flow. The atmosphere is accordingly laidback – if increasingly swish. Witness it for yourself from a table outside Daylesford on Westbourne Grove.

01 **Ally Capellino**
312 Portobello Road W10 5RU
020 8964 1022
allycapellino.co.uk
Mon-Sat 11-6, Sun 11-5

See page 56 for Marylebone shop, page 139 for Shoreditch shop, and pages 58–63 for interview.

02 **Flow**
1-5 Needham Road W11 2RP
020 7243 0782
flowgallery.co.uk
Mon-Sat 11-6, Sun by appointment

Opened by Yvonna Demczynska in 1999, Flow offers an uplifting shopping experience devoid of the clutter and crowds Notting Hill is known for. Demczynska personally seeks out fledgling artists both from the UK and also from abroad, and features the finest works in regular exhibitions themed by material, colour and subject matter.

03 **Heal's**
Queens Building,
Westbourne Grove W2 5AA
0207 896 7451
heals.co.uk
Mon-Sat 9.30-6, Thu 9.30-7, Sun 12-6

A new venture for Heal's, this relatively small store is a boutique alternative to their established flagship on Tottenham Court Road (see page 57). Housed within the art deco splendour of the Queens Building are abundant displays of lighting from a multitude of leading brands including Tom Dixon, Flos, Anglepoise and Terence Woodgate. Due to its size, this store uses digital displays to show off the full Heal's range of furniture, furnishings and fabrics, and a team of interior specialists are available to steer you in the right direction and discuss interior projects, making it an altogether more bespoke shopping experience.

Creative thinker
Carmel Allen,
Heal's

Carmel Allen was a writer and editor before she joined Heal's in 2013 as creative director, via a stint at The Conran Shop as marketing director. She's worked to bring the centuries-old retailer back to its roots as a champion of British craft and design, drawing in gifted young makers like Gareth Neal and Sam Lloyd. She won *Homes & Gardens'* 2015 Retailer of the Year award, and recently launched Heal's latest store, in the historic Queens Building in Westbourne Grove.

Heal's has managed to acquire some landmark real estate for its stores. Tell us about this one.
This was one of the first cinemas in London, a beautiful art deco building. We look at this as a template for a store with a much smaller footprint that still offers a full Heal's service. As a nod to the building's cinematic history, the corner window is a screen that tells a story about what's inside. We've looked at technology used by sports stores like Nike, where people are really engaged, and how we can bring that kind of experience and energy here. Matt Elton, one of our 'Heal's Discovers' designers, has also done elements of the shop fittings. It's predominantly a lighting showroom, with a few furniture pieces below. Whatever's not here is on the screens, and can be delivered to you the next day. We have a full fabric library, and every member of staff is a fully trained stylist, so you can bring your ideas and they can work with your sketches to pull things together.

How did you decide what you would focus on?
Lighting is a really strong category for us, so it made sense to bring light into this area. There's just a nod to the furniture. If we'd brought in all the furniture collections, it would have been too much.

Which designers are you getting behind in 2015?
We worked very closely with David Steiner, who pioneered the Ambrose collection, a reference to Ambrose Heal. It's all about small spaces and smart living. We called it Ambrose because in the 1930s Ambrose designed furniture that was suitable for the new suburban houses. Up until then, no one had designed furniture to that scale. David has also designed a collection called the Dodie, after Dodie Smith, the author of *I Capture the Castle* and *101 Dalmatians*. She had a very long affair with Ambrose Heal and moved to a flat not far from here. When she moved there, she decided she wanted something modern and was going to buy this Italian set of furniture and Ambrose said, 'Absolutely not.' He designed an art deco bedroom set not dissimilar to this Dodie range, which falls into the Ambrose collection.

Do you see this property as expansion or focus?
I see it as focus and growth and embracing change. I often think to myself, 'What would Ambrose do?' He was such a great retailer, always forward thinking but also putting the customer at the centre of everything. If you look at how people shop now, they're doing lots of research online, then making a destination visit to the stores. People lead such busy lives, that when they do come out, there's got to be a good experience for them when they get there. **EH**

02 Heal's Queens Building, Westbourne Grove W2 5AA (See page 35)

Free spirit
Ross Lovegrove

Pioneering industrial designer Ross Lovegrove is rather vague about the place he calls home. His international client base takes him on a constant circuit of the globe, but London, or more specifically Notting Hill, is his base and the location of his studio. We met him for an open discussion on his career evolution and continuing trajectory.

"I worked in Shoreditch for three years in the 1980s. I've been there, done that," laughs Lovegrove, as we talk about the current hotspot for designers in London. After a stint sharing a studio with Jasper Morrison in Ladbroke Grove, he relocated to a studio (and home upstairs) on a rather dodgy mews street in Notting Hill. He spent three years converting it, the most ambitious part being the excavation of the cavernous basement. He recalls the day he moved in, when a bunch of kids outside were playing *Living in the Ghetto* on their boom box. "I'd put all my money into the place. Everything!"

Of course, more than 20 years on and the area has shifted from a rough neighbourhood to a new form of ghetto for the rich and famous. Lovegrove disassociates with this change and struggles with the 'ladies who lunch' reality of today's Westbourne Grove, which he likens to Beverly Hills. This is a man who believes in hard work as a means of existence. Despite his considerable reputation and countless achievements in the design industry, he doesn't suggest the pressure ever eases off.

He was perfectly frank when discussing the challenges of operating a design studio in London. "My fixed overheads increase about 10 per cent a year, so I

04 Museum of Brands, Packaging and Advertising
111–117 Lancaster Road W11 1QT
020 7908 0888
museumofbrands.com
Tues–Sat 10–6, Sun 11–5

Consumer historian Robert Opie sees beauty in big branded merchandise. He brought his vast collection of boxes, tins, magazines and adverts from Gloucester to London 10 years ago to tell the story of our social history. In 2015, the museum moved to larger premises to house a growing collection, also staging ever-changing exhibitions on subjects ranging from wartime labels to royal souvenirs.

05 Native & Co
116 Kensington Park Road W11 2PW
020 7243 0418
nativeandco.com
Tues–Sat 11–6.30, Sun 11–5

Stocking a range of high-quality crafted homewares sourced from Japan and Taiwan, this shop, located with minimal signage next to the established Vessel Gallery (see page 45), is a real gem that will appeal to anyone who has an appreciation for the meticulous care and attention to detail that these cultures so frequently display. Elegant stoneware ceramic mugs sit alongside graphic brass trivets, delicate cedar sake cups, canvas aprons and cast iron kettles. A lot of love has gone into setting up this carefully curated store, and this is mirrored on its website, but one can't help feeling it might be more at home in a different part of town.

06 The Rug Company
124 Holland Park Avenue W11 4UE
020 7908 9990
therugcompany.com
Mon–Sat 10–6, Sun 11–5

Founders Suzanne and Christopher Sharp, known for their successful alliances with designers like Paul Smith, Matthew Williamson and Barber Osgerby, were one of the first

have to increase my turnover by that much just to be in the same place as I was last year. Ultimately, the rising costs in London are not sustainable." Lovegrove boasts a global client list, so I question why he needs to keep his studio in the capital. He ponders the suggestion and agrees that he could be anywhere, that London is a bit of an old antique shop, and that he doesn't need to be located in a design hub. But he counters this by saying, "London pushes you to be successful and part of my success has come from being here. I love the city's cultural scene – the art, the architecture, the museums..."

It is from his London studio that his output has prospered, where he and a team of about six work tirelessly on pushing the capabilities of technology and exploring the limits of materials. Walking around the two floors – interconnected by the studio's signature spiral staircase with a minimally-supported carbon fibre handrail – one can't help but be drawn to a plethora of material samples, 3D-printed trials and prototypes, walls covered in imagery of forms from nature, and other intrigues at every turn. It is from this studio that he has created everything from cutlery and tableware

to lighting, furniture, electronic devices and airline seating, all imbued with a sinuous, ergonomic 'Organic Essentialism', as he calls it.

Lovegrove passionately believes that industrial design is a powerful profession but adds, "Design is still treated like a cheap, accessible commodity and I fundamentally don't believe in this." So what motivates him? "I am motivated by a sincere need to contribute to the quality of our three-dimensional world with design that embodies a spirit of our times. I like to experiment with the tools of our times. I feel the constant pressure to innovate."

At one point in the interview he says, "The future excites me." He is animated by a desire to live in a world that is always several steps ahead of where we are today. And, on reflection, this explains various bouts of negativity that pepper our conversation. One senses that he becomes frequently frustrated and disillusioned by the conservative attitudes and fear of progression that hampers the sort of revolutionary ideas that he would like to implement. In parallel, it is exactly those frustrations that will continue to feed the very genius that is Ross Lovegrove. **MF**

Material man

Tom Dixon,

Tom Dixon Shop

Tom Dixon was welding, potting and woodworking at a time when the UK had largely stopped making. His career springboarded from the self-produced S-Chair, now at MoMA in New York, into collaborations with Italian masters like Achille Castiglioni and Ettore Sottsass, via luxury-brand commissions. In 1998 he took over the design department at Habitat and in 2002 started his own brand, inspired by British history, industry and the thrill of making by hand. We met him at his shop-restaurant complex at Portobello Dock.

Tell us about your history in this neighbourhood.
In the 1970s I went to Holland Park Comprehensive. I had my first pottery lesson there. I did technical and life drawing, and that's probably where it all started. That was at the bottom of Ladbroke Grove and now I'm at the top, in the last remaining ungentrified bit. I started my career welding in the coal cellar of my house in a rough-and-ready part of Notting Hill. I've had about seven studios in the neighbourhood and still have a workshop on All Saints Road. I've always dabbled in retail and commerce – I could never make another piece until I sold the first one. And the idea that someone would buy a load of scrap metal I'd converted into a chair seemed like a brilliant way to make a living.

What brought you back?
I was in my Bloomsbury studio and phoned up several property developers to see if I could find something interesting, and this was the only thing that came up. The developer believed in my potential as an anchor tenant. We started off by filling all the buildings with young designers and having big events here. It became quite a vibrant place. It had been Virgin Records HQ and already had a canteen. I chanced upon a young chef [Stevie Parle] who wanted a small, experimental restaurant, and it grew through its own reputation.

importers to transform underfoot design. Each rug is hand-dyed and hand-knotted from Tibetan wool over several months using traditional rug-making techniques. Their rugs are all here, neatly stacked on shelves in surprising contemporary colours or rolled up with their tassels aloft. Every design comes with a handy postcard to take home and debate over with your partner.

07 SCP West

87 Westbourne Grove W2 4UL
020 7229 3612
scp.co.uk
Mon-Sat 9.30-6, Sun 11-5

This end of Westbourne Grove is peppered with various stores selling interior products. Thankfully, SCP's low glass box of a store is a welcome contributor, albeit only a fraction of the size of its Shoreditch parent (see page 150). It caters for the burgeoning appetite for contemporary design on this side of the city. The stock differs too, with more emphasis on smaller items and giftware, as well as choice items of furniture and a tight edit of lighting. SCP has more than 30 years of experience in the industry so you're in the best hands.

08 Themes & Variations

231 Westbourne Grove W11 2SE
020 7727 5531
themesandvariations.com
Mon-Fri 10-1, 2-6, Sat 10-6

Back in the early 1980s, dealer Liliane Fawcett took a gamble on this area's economic arrival and it paid off. She was responsible for bringing European contemporary postwar furniture and decorative arts to the UK and this is where Piero Fornasetti first made his name in London design circles. It's also the place to find Fontana Arte floor lamps, Gio Ponti wing chairs and Cedric Ragot vases. Thankfully, the space isn't crammed– the careful edit bringing an air of calm and sophistication to enable its gems to really shine.

> "
> ***I've liked building something big and multidimensional enough to survive in a tertiary location. People come because we've created a more interesting infrastructure than just a shop.***
> "

Has occupying down-at-heel buildings informed your design?
This place has that historic subtext that I'm fascinated by. I love how the canal is connected to the Port of London and the industrial North. It's a beautiful network. The building has allowed us to spread out in a way that's difficult to do in London. I've liked building something big and multidimensional enough to survive in a tertiary location. People come because we've created a more interesting infrastructure than just a shop. The only irritation for me is that we've run out of space to do something else. If I had my way, we'd colonise the water, have a bit of manufacturing, and offer other brands.

How do you think that things have changed for makers since you first started out?
Just like in the music business, where you used to need a 48-track studio and a big company to back you, now you can send a file from your laptop to an engineer who's got a digitally controlled tool to convert it. You can have things coming out in small, medium or large numbers in a way that was inconceivable for me at the time. I'm talking about sheet metal-pressing, laser-cutting, CNC-turning – things that are made by computer-controlled machines now. A really high-tech, heavy industry is accessible to every designer, and not everybody realises that.

You have this amazing prescience for what materials are going to be desired. How do you know?
I get bored easily – probably slightly earlier than some other people. Also, we have to become obsessed with something other people aren't doing, otherwise we can't compete in terms of scale. When I arrived at Habitat I studied all the different cycles since 1964. I've always liked museums as well, where you get a sense of the cycles that happen. Tracking copper, for instance: I saw that it was popular in arts and crafts and the 1960s, and it was weird that nobody else had been using it, because it's such a great colour.

Can you choose something in the store that encapsulates what you're trying to do now?
I'm never satisfied with anything that I do, to be honest. But I like the Melt light because it's so recognisably ours. The mould is a ready-made one that belongs to the Swedish design collective Front, but we managed to make something out of it that's completely different. So that was... satisfactory. EH

07 Tom Dixon Shop
Wharf Building, Portobello Dock, 344 Ladbroke Grove W10 5BU (See right)

09 Tom Dixon Shop
Wharf Building, Portobello Dock,
344 Ladbroke Grove W10 5BU
020 7183 9737
tomdixon.net
Mon-Sat 10-6, Sun 11-5

The designer's stamp is all over the London design trail, but Tom Dixon's converted-warehouse boutique, north of Notting Hill proper, is worth the crawl. Dark and broody, the canalside showroom glows from the designer's trendsetting metallic lighting and newer glass pendants, each hand-cast with a unique iridescent sheen. His furniture collection is here too: impossibly smooth wood seating and upholstered pieces with art deco curves. They're styled against metallic vessels and giftware, plus inspiring items from fellow designers that Dixon curates with a gallerist's eye. Since you're making the trip, book a table at the Dock Kitchen, headed up by chef Stevie Parle and furnished, naturally, with the landlord's own creations. (See left and pages 42–44)

10 Vessel Gallery
114 Kensington Park Road
W11 2PW
020 7727 8001
vesselgallery.com
Mon-Sat 10-6

The vast and complicated glass and ceramic-art worlds are rarely seen, even by dedicated gallery hoppers, but Vessel gets to the heart of them, showing statement-making pieces by industry legends such as Oiva Toikka, Lena Bergström and Jeremy Maxwell Wintrebert, as well as emerging talents, bringing an element of added value to the snug space. The gallery has also helped more mainstream artists launch niche collections, including Jaime Hayon and his Japanese-style tableware. The company operates a growing contract business, popular with architects and interior designers. The space might be small but the knowledge and service is expert, making a visit here second to none.

For low-key burgers
11 Electric Diner
191 Portobello Road W11 2ED
020 7908 9696
electricdiner.com

At this American-style diner-in-a-tunnel, you can enjoy a mean burger and fries in a bright red banquette. It's a good spot for watching the Notting Hillbillies strut their stuff.

For an evening pick-me-up
12 Goode & Wright
271 Portobello Road W11 1LR
020 7727 5552
goodeandwright.co.uk

A wood-panelled French bistro that offers terrific aperitifs, plus sprightly plates of crab, marrowbone on toast and buttermilk fried quail to share.

For classy eggs
13 Granger & Co
175 Westbourne Grove W11 2SB
020 7229 9111
grangerandco.com

Take champagne with your eggs Benedict or add it to your kale and cucumber juice. It also offers superb bread made on the premises, and an uplifting yellow and marble-heavy interior.

For modern British dinner
14 Hereford Road
3 Hereford Road W2 4AB
020 7727 1144
herefordroad.org

This dependably good restaurant has a no-nonsense approach to ingredients. Décor is similarly laidback, featuring white tiles and red leather banquettes overlooking the kitchen.

For sophisticated lunch
15 The Ledbury
127 Ledbury Road W11 2AQ
020 7792 9090
theledbury.com

A two-Michelin-starred restaurant that draws in diners from around the world for its elegant approach to fine cooking using the best ingredients. Design is smart and stark; expect white tablecloths and heavy curtains.

For dependable breakfast
16 Pizza East
310 Portobello Road W10 5TA
020 8969 4500
pizzaeast.com/portobello

This pared-back pizza joint also does a healthy breakfast trade. Dabble in a Bloody Mary with green eggs (English muffin with ham, poached eggs and pesto).

For pre-dinner spritz
17 Polpo
126–128 Notting Hill Gate W11 3QG
020 7229 3283
polpo.co.uk

A bustier version of the Soho original with warm lighting and clay paintwork. Bring friends for several Aperol spritzes and platefuls of Italian snacks, especially the moreish stuffed olives.

For filling grub
18 The Shed
122 Palace Gardens Terrace W8 4RT
020 7229 4024
theshed-restaurant.com

This is a very snug space with tractor and motor parts and cow prints adorning the walls. Locals really like the English wine and innovative meaty dishes. Be careful, though, as the tempting dishes means the bill can soon rack up.

For a Scandi lunch
19 Snaps + Rye
93 Golborne Road W10 5NL
020 8964 3004
snapsandrye.com

Snaps + Rye delights with its minimal, bright and pleasing décor, delicious Danish smørrebrød and waitresses with a wry sense of humour. Make sure you buy some Lakrids.

For morning joy
20 Talkhouse Coffee
275 Portobello Road W11 1LR
020 7221 8992
talkhousecoffee.com

A minimally designed, elegant wood and white Scandinavian coffee house with an equally minimal menu: just espresso, filter coffee, hot chocolate and pastries. Expect to be cheered up by knowledgeable baristas who like putting smiley faces on their coffee art.

BOOK A ROOM

For neighbourhood townhouse
21 The Laslett
8 Pembridge Gardens W2 4DU
020 3474 4140
thelaslett.co.uk

For minimalist calm
22 La Suite West
41–51 Inverness Terrace W2 3JN
020 7313 8484
lasuitewest.com

Opposite, tea for two in one of The Laslett's suites

DAILY SPECIALS
BROAD BEAN + MINT SOUP
FETA, PARSLEY +
BULGUR WHEAT
FISH
PEAS
PASTRIES

London property:

From houses to homes… to deposit boxes

London is one of the most frenzied and important property markets in the world. It is also the easy focus for discontent about a less inclusive, money-driven city. Bit by bit, London is becoming about upmarket restaurants, global retail chains, coffee shops and slick office space – but most of all, about speculative property development.

A key factor behind London's frothy property prices is its status as a global magnet for questionably gained money laundered through its upmarket properties via offshore companies. This has driven up average prices with a ripple effect down the price chain, enabling millions of pounds to be "deposited" in London's bricks and mortar, facilitated by Britain's notoriously lax rules on property ownership disclosure.

This scenario is skewing property developers towards building high-priced flats and houses rather than ones ordinary people can afford. And while London's luxury property money sloshes in, there seems to be little political incentive to improve Londoners' lives by providing affordable housing.

As a result of the upward spiral of London's property prices, an increasing number of people now make up London's growing rental market, which is having wide-reaching effects – most notably the delay in putting down roots or having children.

London's housing shortage, coupled with a shortfall of affordable housing, is further exacerbated by a growing population, in part boosted by immigration. This is becoming one of London's defining challenges: if it becomes too expensive to live in London, why would businesses come here? If London employers aren't able to meet salary expectations for the best talent, particularly to accommodate the high cost of living in the capital, will London start witnessing a brain drain? Radical new housing solutions are needed – and fast.

Yet social engineering in London has existed for a long time. Many professionals and City workers have found it necessary over the years to move out of London to find a home, particularly when they started families. One might question why it is fair and acceptable to enable those in social housing to live in London with the taxpayers footing the bill while the very same tax payers are forced to move elsewhere to make a home? Increasingly, only two groups look set to be able to live in London – the very rich and those in social housing.

For those starting out in London as students, going to university is becoming an elitist activity due to high fees and debt – never mind the cost of living. This is further compounded by the influx of foreign students, competing for London's limited housing supply.

With education becoming commoditised, the boom in new university complexes, along with purpose-built accommodation, is resulting in cookie-cutter 'patchwork' facade blocks blighting London's landscape, their proliferation fuelled by property investors.

As a leading global centre for the creative industries, it is questionable how London will be able to continue supporting and sustaining young grass-roots talent, which so crucially gives this city its reputation.

Many young adults have no option but to stay living at the family home (if they're lucky enough to have parents still living in or around London) or share houses in parts of London that have yet to be gentrified or the capital's outer zones. Others are giving up on London altogether, giving rise to the growth in second-tier UK cities, such as Leeds, Birmingham and Manchester – which is perhaps no bad thing, given the over-emphasis on London for the UK's economic recovery.

Yet London is still the most popular capital in Europe to launch a start-up, largely due to it being the home of every conceivable type of industry, combined with its international and diverse population. Creative/tech clusters featuring large buildings of housing for rent with built-in coworking centres could well be the future.

the great divide

Buying into London's property boom may get you a slice of the pie, but it's slowly losing its flavour

London's existing property stock is also under attack, thanks to a relaxing of the planning regulations required to convert commercial buildings into residential use. The results of this can be seen all over the city, with developers and landlords cashing in on the strong demand for residential properties, forcing out local stores, music venues and businesses in the process.

From the creative corners of Soho and Shoreditch to the cosy confines of Highgate and Chelsea, the aggressive pace of gentrification is turning districts into boring shadows of their former selves which only tourists think are interesting or edgy.

One by-product of London's property bonanza is that the city seems to be in the grip of a profit-driven puritanism, marked by an unsavoury cocktail of councils too blind to see what really makes cities great; developers using legal clout, poor planning laws and cosy relationships to bulldoze anything in their way; and wealthy dullards who think they have bought themselves a slice of London cool, only to find that the "coolness" has moved on.

This is because those who can actually afford central London districts (financiers and the international super-rich) may say that they love cool London, but in truth they can't bear the reality – the noise, the rubbish and the riff-raff. What they really want is a kind of Singapore with Georgian houses. They like high-end chains, expensive eateries and upmarket interiors shops – the latter of which are springing up to cater for them (Italian brands are especially good at providing safe cafe-au-lait coloured furnishings, usually vast in scale, and state-of-the-art kitchens).

Property developers need to remember that London's creative and night-time economy is a huge part of what makes London such a dynamic and vibrant place to live and work in. Its bars, restaurants, museums and theatres have been major drivers behind the renaissance in urban living.

Tower block to power block

What a difference three decades makes. In the 1990s, 'high-rise' was associated with unloved council flats, broken lifts and blocked rubbish chutes. Fast forward to 2015 and tower block means power block, with expensive privately-owned sky pads.

London is in the grip of a construction explosion, with more than 200 towers on the drawing board across London, translating to approximately 18,000 high-rise apartments, with a further 70,000 in the pipeline. Many of these are planned for London's riversides. Poorly designed and executed in contrast to the City's office skyscrapers, one of London's most renowned town planners, Peter Rees, famously dubbed them "a slum for the rich".

These high-rise homes are outside the price range of most, now that London property prices per square foot are the second highest in the world* after Monaco. As the hoardings come down off each building site, declaring cliches like "The true marque of prestigious living" and "Connected like no other", it's another step towards London becoming a tame Disneyland for grown-ups.

* London School of Economics' Centre for Economic Performance

Capital city: fluid and flexible

Once upon a time, London's postcodes were known for being inhabited by certain groups: Hampstead had intellectuals; Islington had media types; Camden had goths and punks; Fulham had toffs who couldn't afford Chelsea; Notting Hill had its hillbillies; and Chelsea had rich folk. Today, all of these districts are just for the rich. The parts of London that have traditionally been for the wealthy – Mayfair, Belgravia and Kensington – have moved up to the ultra-prime level – only affordable to wealthy foreigners who live abroad. These absentee homeowners are creating ghost towns in central London, causing local businesses to close. Meanwhile, London's well-off middle classes are being pushed into London's Zone 2, pushing the cool kids and creatives into Zone 3 and beyond.

One bright spot is that London's property issues are bringing people together who are acquiring a heightened feeling of community spirit. Residents are doing battle with developers, and in some cases stopping areas being sold off-plan to investors as "Monopoly board investments".

It wasn't that long ago that today's hipster hotspots – Dalston, Brixton and King's Cross – were rundown, no-go areas. London's architects, interior designers, design retailers and furniture makers are benefitting from the capital's regeneration, whether it's collaborating on residential and commercial projects or creating bespoke commissions. This is enabling designers to stay in London and expand their studios while playing a part in the city's creative community. Long considered the design capital of the world, London's wealth of design talent to draw upon is a compelling component of its property scene.

London is fluid and flexible, and thankfully not preserved in aspic like Paris or an artificial construct like Dubai. Londoners are doing what they have always done – being resourceful and inventive – colonising new areas and carving out new cultural zones away from the tourist throngs.

London has changed since the financial crisis – not only in spirit but also in form. Progress needs change and it is progress that keeps London at the top of its game and top of the list of most desirable places to live and work. Property, tourism, finance and food (where London is a victim of its own success) is the price to pay for being the pre-eminent metropolis on the globe.

Yvonne Courtney is a design PR strategist – brokering designers with the media, manufacturers, gallerists and retailers – and a design commentator, lobbyist and writer.

MARYLEBONE & FITZROVIA

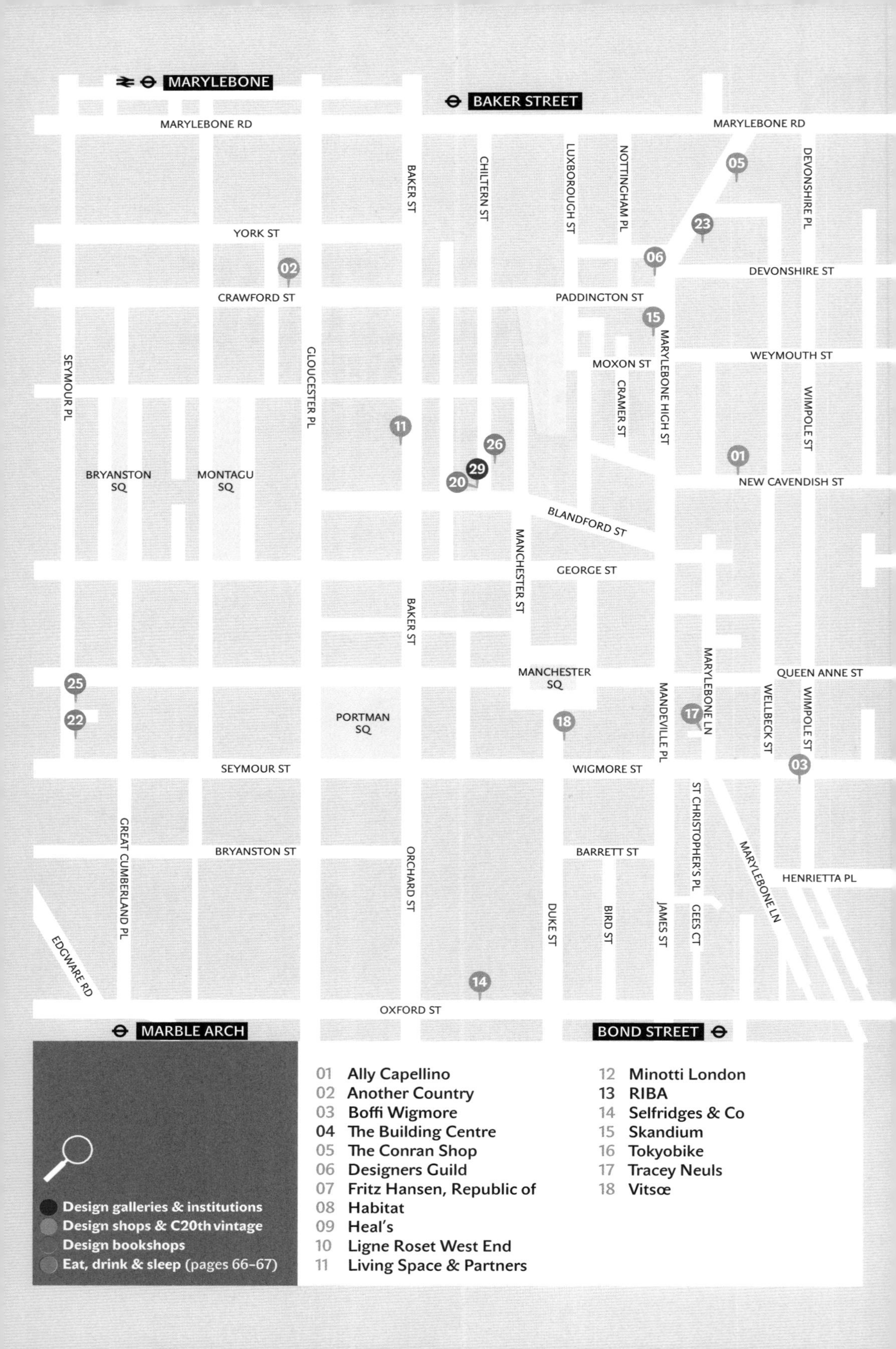
MARYLEBONE
BAKER STREET
MARYLEBONE RD
MARYLEBONE RD
BAKER ST
CHILTERN ST
LUXBOROUGH ST
NOTTINGHAM PL
DEVONSHIRE PL
YORK ST
DEVONSHIRE ST
CRAWFORD ST
PADDINGTON ST
MARYLEBONE HIGH ST
WEYMOUTH ST
MOXON ST
CRAMER ST
SEYMOUR PL
GLOUCESTER PL
WIMPOLE ST
BRYANSTON SQ
MONTAGU SQ
NEW CAVENDISH ST
BLANDFORD ST
MANCHESTER ST
GEORGE ST
BAKER ST
MANCHESTER SQ
QUEEN ANNE ST
MARYLEBONE LN
WELLBECK ST
WIMPOLE ST
MANDEVILLE PL
PORTMAN SQ
SEYMOUR ST
WIGMORE ST
ST CHRISTOPHER'S PL
GREAT CUMBERLAND PL
BRYANSTON ST
ORCHARD ST
BARRETT ST
MARYLEBONE LN
HENRIETTA PL
DUKE ST
BIRD ST
JAMES ST
GEES CT
EDGWARE RD
OXFORD ST
MARBLE ARCH
BOND STREET
Design galleries & institutions
Design shops & C20th vintage
Design bookshops
Eat, drink & sleep (pages 66–67)
01 Ally Capellino
02 Another Country
03 Boffi Wigmore
04 The Building Centre
05 The Conran Shop
06 Designers Guild
07 Fritz Hansen, Republic of
08 Habitat
09 Heal's
10 Ligne Roset West End
11 Living Space & Partners
12 Minotti London
13 RIBA
14 Selfridges & Co
15 Skandium
16 Tokyobike
17 Tracey Neuls
18 Vitsœ

Marylebone & Fitzrovia

Covent Garden & Holborn p92 ↗

↓ Mayfair & Soho p72

Historically, landed gentry settled around the squares of Marylebone, while in Fitzrovia were the intelligentsia of University of London and later, workers for the garment industry. Their legacy is a diverse shopping district with an international inflection: marble tables from Italy, midcentury modernism from Scandinavia and slouchy sofas from France. Newcomers like Another Country and Ally Capellino join Habitat and Heal's as best of British.

01 Ally Capellino
11 New Cavendish Street W1G 9UD
020 7224 0648
allycapellino.co.uk
Mon–Sat 10–6, Sun 11–5

This is the third and newest London store from bag and accessories designer Alison Lloyd, aka Ally Capellino. She has made a name for herself designing timeless and hard-wearing bags for everyday use, embracing the functional needs of working men and women without over-embellishment and fuss. Bags for all occasions can be found here, giving her loyal following reason to come back for more. (See pages 58–63)

02 Another Country
18 Crawford Street W1H 1BT
020 7486 3251
anothercountry.com
Mon–Fri 10–6, Sat 11–5

Contemporary furniture has been moving toward a simpler, more functional aesthetic for years, but few people have brought out lines so simple they bring to mind Shaker, Japanese craft and Scandinavian modern. Five years ago, former magazine publisher Paul de Zwart had a hunch it would sell and now, barely a year since he opened a standalone store on this pretty, villagey street in Marylebone, he's growing. Give yourself two minutes here and you'll rue your cluttered, complicated existence at home and yearn to start fresh. Then you'll splurge on Common Goods dish soap (from £11) and plan your purge. (See pages 64–65)

03 Boffi Wigmore
25 Wigmore Street W1U 1PN
020 7629 0058
boffiuk.com
Mon–Sat 9.30–5.30

We don't include the 'permanents' for the home – kitchens and bathrooms – in this guide, but we make an exception here as this showroom is worth a look for the fantasy alone. Boffi alters perceptions of what a kitchen should be, thanks to designer Piero Lissoni, who has spent decades ensuring the brand is the nonpareil of utilitarian design.

04 The Building Centre
26 Store Street WC1E 7BT
020 7692 4000
buildingcentre.co.uk
Mon–Fri 9–6, Sat 10–5

This builders' resource centre, in a glorious Beaux Arts building, keeps track of the city's built developments and offers advice, information and support to the industry. For the layperson, there is a continually updated scale model of central London, building material displays, and a continual programme of informative exhibitions that often have a focus on London and its ever-expanding built environment.

05 The Conran Shop
55–57 Marylebone High Street
W1U 5HS
020 7723 2223
conranshop.co.uk
Mon–Sat 10–7, Sun 11–6

The Conran Shop founder Terence Conran is the godfather of contemporary design retail in Britain. Son Jasper is now creative director and can be thanked for

The Conran Shop

sustaining his father's vision and adding an injection of energy that makes the stores so appealing.

06 Designers Guild

76 Marylebone High Street W1U 5JU
020 3301 5826
designersguild.com
Mon-Sat 10-6, Thurs 10-7, Sun 11-5

Designers Guild's linens, wallpapers and upholsteries are colourful and floral but have an uncanny modernity. The expansive King's Road flagship (page 16) is a rush – it hits you from all directions. This one grows on you more subtly but stick with it. You'll start to get the colour combinations, rethink your bathroom scheme and possibly even find a deal.

07 Fritz Hansen, Republic of

13 Margaret Street W1W 8RN
020 7637 5534
fritzhansen.com
Mon-Sat 10- 6.30, Thurs 10-7, Sun 10- 5

To put its furnishings in homely context, Danish brand Fritz Hansen teamed up with like-minded crowd-pleaser Skandium to launch this Scandi extravaganza. So you get the Arne Jacobsen oeuvre and the range of timeless Poul Kjaerholm tables teamed with Louis Poulsen pendant lights and giant Rosendahl monkeys.

08 Habitat

196–199 Tottenham Court Road W1T 7PJ
0344 499 1122
habitat.co.uk
Mon-Sat 10-7, Thurs 10-8, Sun 12-6

Through the turn of the millennium, Habitat's blend of affordable simplicity and mind-blowing colour was irresistible. But like so many good things, it was impossible to sustain. In 2011, the company launched by Terence Conran in 1964 lost all but three of its UK stores. The brand was acquired by Argos-owner Home Retail Group and chugged along with mediocre product. Now the company hopes it'll be the comeback story of 2015, as it concentrates on opening as many as 80 mini-stores across the country, filling them with new homegrown design.

09 Heal's

The Heal's Building, 196 Tottenham Court Road W1T 7LQ
020 7636 1666
heals.co.uk
Mon-Sat 10-7, Thurs 10-8, Sun 12-6

At more than 200 years old, this is the eminent grise of Tottenham Court Road's design community. Acknowledging that there is no space for complacency in retail today, Heal's has gone to great lengths to overhaul its flagship and give it the upmarket vibe it deserves. Its prominent window displays and main entrance foyer gallery are always worth a look.

10 Ligne Roset West End

23/25 Mortimer Street W1T 3JE
020 7323 1248
ligne-roset.co.uk
Mon-Sat 10-6, Thurs 10-8, Sun 12-5

Ligne Roset's West End showroom is an upside-down version of its City location (page 145), extending over the main and basement levels of this petite space. As such, the collection on show is highly edited, showing only the latest ranges in the most covetable new colours.

11 Living Space & Partners

55 Baker Street W1U 8EW
020 7486 0311
livingspaceuk.com
Mon-Sat 9.30-6; Sun 12-5

Living Space is a design showroom for those on the hunt for slick furniture and clever systems to free up your space. Their repertoire includes not just shelving systems and barely-there bed frames but a complete range of interior architecture. Staff are on hand to assist with suggestions and a more detailed design service to bring the right configuration to your home.

A meeting of minds

A meeting of minds

Tracey Neuls & Ally Capellino

Tracey Neuls and Alison Lloyd (aka Ally) both studied fashion but that's not all that they have in common. These two independent designers launched their respective businesses in 2000. They both opened their first stores in 2005, then their second stores in 2011. Neuls designs shoes, Lloyd designs bags and accessories, and yet, despite both designing items that adorn the human body, they consider themselves more closely aligned to product than fashion. Both women are relaxed when we meet for tea opposite Ally Capellino's newest shop on New Cavendish Street in Marylebone (see page 56), a short walk from Neuls' original premises on Marylebone Lane (see page 63). Both characters are instantly likeable: Canadian-born Neuls, with her fiery red hair and signature tuft, is all smiles and laughs; British-born Lloyd is more restrained, albeit with an underlying dry humour. They chat comfortably together, comparing stories and updating each other on recent happenings.

These are both women with a confident sense of belonging. They run their businesses as they see best,

Opposite, Tracey Neuls' shop on Marylebone Lane

Above, Capellino's New Cavendish Street shop

without compromise from outside influences. Their loyal customers buy into them as talented individuals and treasure their purchases for years at a time. Crucially for both, there is nothing overly precious about their products, nor are they trying to define a "look". Instead, they want you to use and wear their products every day; make them a part of your own personal style; allow them to age naturally and take on a worn patina.

Despite the demands of their burgeoning businesses, both still design from scratch and work closely with their suppliers to realise their vision. Neuls purposely avoids looking at other fashion, drawing her influences from further afield. This is Lloyd's approach too, although she likes to keep an eye on what's happening in the fashion arena. Both avoid unnecessary design embellishments and garish branding, preferring to ensure fit, comfort, practicality and discretion.

"I am a practical type," states Lloyd. "I always like things that leave me hands-free, that you can put things in, but that don't weigh too much." She's referring to her bags that are made from hard-wearing materials that become more beautiful with use. She often chooses to combine two fabrics and has a penchant for waxed cotton that features with leather straps and handles. Describing the attributes of her bags, she says, "Good leather and materials, not flashy, pared-down and quite often very simply put together so that you can understand the architecture of the piece."

Neuls tends to treat her shoe designs rather like a sculpture for the foot. The child in her loves designing straight into plasticine, instantly bringing to life forms in her brain via her hands. Indeed, forms she sculpted at the start of her business still feature today, including the comfortable Geek shoe with its pronounced sole. Her heeled shoes have curvaceous details that can only be attributed to Tracey Neuls. She also does a range for men and a range for cycling.

"We have customers who grow old with their shoes, rather than bored with them," she declares proudly. There are no age boundaries either – she's at her happiest when mother and daughter shop together in her stores. These spaces – the original in Marylebone and the second in Shoreditch – are

---

12 Minotti London
77 Margaret Street W1W 8SY
020 7323 3233
minottilondon.com
Mon–Fri 9.30–6, Sat 10–6

Italian furniture brand Minotti's magnificent London headquarters, located on the raised ground floor of a polished heritage mansion block in Fitzrovia, allows visitors to inspect the fine detail in the finishes and upholsteries, subtle features that are impossible to pick up online.

13 RIBA
66 Portland Place W1B 1AD
020 7580 5533
architecture.com
Mon–Fri 9.30–5.30, Sat 10–5

Few buildings in London are more inspiring than the George Grey Wornum-designed home of the Royal Institute of British Architects. It features a café and bookshop, two exhibition spaces showing a roster of insightful installations, and a library of almost Oxbridge magnificence.

14 Selfridges & Co
400 Oxford Street W1A 1AB
0800 123400
selfridges.com
Mon–Sat 9.30–9, Sun 11.30–6.15

Selfridges has undoubtedly moved forward under the creative directorship of Alannah Weston, but try not to go on a weekend. If you do wind up here on a mad Saturday afternoon, hunt out pockets of calm in this monolithic building (such as the fourth floor furniture department) or relax with a glass of vino in Harry Gordon's basement wine bar.

15 Skandium
86 Marylebone High St W1U 4QS
020 7935 2077
skandium.com
Mon–Sat 10–18:30, Thurs 10–7, Sun 11–5

Despite plenty of competition, Skandium is king of the Scandinavian retailers. The ever-expanding enterprise defined who's who in the Scandi canon and continues to set the standard with the best new products from

treated like installations (often by collaboration) and the experience of shopping in them is of paramount importance to her. "My shoes hang from the ceiling to celebrate the detail. It's like a sculpture, and you want to see every angle possible. Fashion is theatrical, and so are the shoes, which is why I present them in this dramatic way."

Talking of their shops, they selected Marylebone and Shoreditch independently of each other (Ally Capellino also has a third store on Portobello Road), but were attracted to the areas for their strong feeling of community. They still boast a good mix of independent and specialist businesses, from small boutiques and galleries to cafés, pubs and restaurants, as well as residential dwellings. Their customers are often drawn to these areas too, preferring to shun the homogeneity of the high street.

Both designers feel despair for the property boom that London is experiencing and the greed that goes with it. As it is for all independent retailers, survival is often at the mercy of opportunistic landlords. They fear that shopping streets will become the reserve of the big brands but, nimble and versatile as they are, these two would simply move if they had to. And yes, their customers would no doubt go with them. **MF**

01 **Ally Capellino**
11 New Cavendish Street W1G 9UD
(See page 56)

17 **Tracey Neuls**
29 Marylebone Lane W1U 2NQ
(See below)

---

the region. It also redefined retail with its open-plan white-walled spaces flooded with natural light from all aspects.

16 **Tokyobike**
14 Eastcastle Street W1T 3AX
020 7636 8240
tokyobike.co.uk
Mon-Fri 11-7, Sat 11-5

See page 150 for Shoreditch shop and further information.

17 **Tracey Neuls**
29 Marylebone Lane W1U 2NQ
020 7935 0039
traceyneuls.com
Mon-Fri 11-6.30, Sat-Sun 12-5

She may be a cobbler but Tracey Neuls is as well known in London as some furniture designers. Her Marylebone boutique (and Shoreditch outpost) has become a fixture on the Design Festival circuit for her collaborations with design-world names like Tord Boontje, Moroso and Retrouvius. Even left to her own devices, Neuls' space is a surreal fantasy world. She was one of the first retailers to display wares from the ceiling, dangling her sculptural shoes from undetectable wires for 360-degree viewing. (See pages 58–63)

18 **Vitsœ**
3-5 Duke Street W1U 3ED
020 7428 1606
vitsoe.com
Mon-Sat 10-6

It's been 50 years since Dieter Rams designed his 606 Universal Shelving System for Vitsœ, the godfather of modular furnishings, but nothing since has ever come close to its style and efficacy. Managing to look both cool and functional for an office and warm and decorative for a lounge, the system is perfection on rails. Which is why the company's Duke Street showrooms are busy from open until close. Staff are as much architects as retailers, and are as open to the possibilities of their product as they are intensely familiar with it.

Lasting power
Paul de Zwart, *Another Country*

Five years ago, the entrepreneur and former *Wallpaper publisher Paul de Zwart designed a few simple furnishings sharing the values of Scandinavian modern, Shaker and Japanese craft. Launching them as Another Country, he expanded the business with two additional furniture series, collections for Heal's and projects for Knole House and the Ditchling Museum of Art & Craft in Sussex. In the year since de Zwart opened the brand's first boutique on Crawford Street in Marylebone, Another Country has grown by 50 per cent.**

You sowed the seeds of this company after years in magazine publishing. Where did it all start?
I was working on a start-up that never started, an operator for high-quality holiday rentals. I was furnishing a property we were using as a model and wanted to find something that would sit comfortably in a rural landscape but had an urbane sensibility. I wanted the perfect stool and I just couldn't find it. Either it cost a lot of money or it was disposable.

Another Country first appeared online with a wholesale element. Why was opening a bricks-and-mortar presence the next logical step for you?
People relate best to our values when they can touch the furniture, see the quality, appreciate that it's made locally or in Europe and develop a personal rapport with the furniture. It's all Grade-A timbers, sustainably harvested, and we design in a way that's contemporarily relevant, but not in a way that's too trendified. Seeing it all together hopefully feels quite consistent. When you see our ceramics, you understand why our tables and textiles are the way they are.

Where does the name Another Country come from?
Back in the 1990s we witnessed a reorganisation of our city – young professionals moving to London, a trend toward urbanisation, a buoyant time economically. Then we grew older, we wanted to escape the city and the whole boutique hotel thing exploded. As we became parents, we had to make different choices. Country has since become closer to us emotionally – also in terms of being aware of where our food grows. The whole aesthetic of country-house hotels has been prevelant. To me, it was obvious we were speaking to people who sit comfortably in a country house setting as well as in their city apartment. I wanted to use the word 'country' – I remember liking a collection by Ineke Hans called 'Neo Country'. We started playing with it from there.

What brought you to Marylebone?
I wanted to be in a part of town that wasn't overly defined by its cultural connotation. I wanted something central. In the east, we would have been very quickly labelled as a happening east London brand, but I wanted the brand to define itself rather than its geography in the city.

How much of the Another Country aesthetic is you personally and how much is the people you employ?
It all began with Stool 1 and its proportions. Our first collection, Series One, was inspired by a Belgian light-wood aesthetic and Nordic interior architecture, which I like a lot. That collection grew out of the basic dimensions and proportions of the stool. It expresses what we stand for in the simplest and most honest way. It doesn't shout at you. It says, 'I'm made of beautiful, long-lasting solid oak timber and I'll always be easy to live with and practical at the same time.'

We design 90 per cent of our furniture in-house with Marie Dessuant, our head of design. We turn to other designers for accessories, lighting, ceramics and textiles. But to celebrate our fifth anniversary, we commissioned five designers to design small furniture and objects inspired by the county of Dorset, where our workshop is. It's the first time we've presented a curated studio collection. EH

02 Another Country 18 Crawford Street W1H 1BT
(See page 56)

Above, the glamorous Berners Tavern dining room

Right, a warm American welcome at The Lockhart

Eat, drink & sleep

For an impressive breakfast

19 Berners Tavern
10 Berners Street W1T 3LF
020 7908 7979
bernerstavern.com

At Jason Atherton's glamorous dining room at The London EDITION hotel, breakfast on grilled kippers with herb butter, avocado on toast or Clarence Court eggs. Book a central booth and gaze up at endless paintings, hung as if in an 18th-century salon.

For a star-spotting dinner

20 Chiltern Firehouse
1 Chiltern Street W1U 7PA
020 7073 7676
chilternfirehouse.com

This New York-style brasserie, headed up by Nuno Mendes, features an open kitchen, cream furnishings, and huge mirrors so you can kick back and relax into an evening of eating crab doughnuts and spying on the celebrity diners.

For a fragrant lunch

21 Dabbous
39 Whitfield Street WIT 2SF
020 7323 1544
dabbous.co.uk

The stern industrial chic of this Michelin-starred restaurant (pronounced Daboo) has been replicated badly elsewhere. Experience the original over a reasonably priced set lunch menu including home-cured goose with fenugreek.

For drinks and pintxos

22 Donostia
10 Seymour Place W1H 7ND
020 3620 1845
donostia.co.uk

Donostia (the Basque word for San Sebastian) is an upmarket tapas bar sporting a minimalist white interior with wooden panelling and a marble bar. Try classic Basque dishes like crispy croquettas or fried cod cheeks with black squid ink aioli.

For Viennese breakfast
23 Fischer's
50 Marylebone High St W1U 5HN
020 7466 5501
fischers.co.uk

This Austrian cafe is a bit like being inside a grand European railway station – you could even dine under the clock. It's the place for Viennese coffee, pastries, and plates of hot gröstl.

For cosy lunch
24 Honey & Co
25A Warren Street W1T 5LZ
020 7388 6175
honeyandco.co.uk

Honey & Co is a welcoming café-restaurant run by a loveable husband-and-wife team who make wonderful baked goods. Order a Middle Eastern salad or Persian chicken dumplings in a fragrant broth.

For cornmeal bread
25 The Lockhart
22–24 Seymour Place W1H 7NL
020 3011 5400
lockhartlondon.com

There's plenty to enjoy at this restaurant that specialises in food of the American South. If you only eat the sticky, sweet, salty hot cornbread, you will be very happy indeed, but carnivores can revel in offerings of southern fried chicken, short ribs and smoked pork belly.

For chic coffee
26 Monocle Café
18 Chiltern Street W1U 7QA
020 7135 2040
café.monocle.com

A stylish, corrugated wood and white painted café, owned by the same-named global magazine, this is perfect for a quick coffee and a pastry – or an important meeting.

For drinks
27 Newman Street Tavern
48 Newman Street W1T 1QQ
020 3667 1445
newmanstreettavern.co.uk

This upmarket gastro pub is just the place for a local evening drink, with its homely, bottle-green interior, friendly staff, impressive wine list and bar snacks.

For upmarket dinner
28 Portland
113 Great Portland Street W1W 6QQ
020 7436 3261
portlandrestaurant.co.uk

Minimal with comfortable touches, from handwritten cloakroom tags to restful velvet banquettes and plenty of space between tables, Portland serves up superb British dishes with an Asian twist.

BOOK A ROOM

For private house service
29 Chiltern Firehouse
1 Chiltern Street W1U 7PA
020 7073 7690
chilternfirehouse.com

For landmark living
30 The London EDITION
10 Berners Street W1T 3NP
020 7781 0000
editionhotels.com/london

Perfect match

Jason Atherton, *Social Wine & Tapas*

Jason Atherton is the Gordon Ramsay-trained chef- patron of restaurant group The Social Company, comprising Michelin-starred restaurants Pollen Street Social and City Social, as well as Berners Tavern at The London EDITION hotel and Typing Room at Bethnal Green's Town Hall Hotel. Next year he plans to open a Japanese-inspired restaurant in the Nova complex in Victoria, while his latest venture, Social Wine & Tapas, on James Street, is a collaboration with sommelier Laure Patry. The restaurant serves a menu of small plates created by Atherton and his head chef, Frankie Van Loo, using British produce.

Do you remember your first taste of wine?
Food came first for me and then it was a natural progression as a good wine really complements a dish. I think my first taste was a sneaky one at a family meal when I was in my teens – I didn't much care for it back then. I had a lot to learn.

How long had you been planning the wine bar, and why did you go down that route?
My executive sommelier Laure Patry wanted to open her own wine bar for some time. Laure and I have worked together for many years now and I wanted to help her, so I proposed adding food to the wine bar; it is very much Laure's restaurant.

Why Marylebone?
It's a busy location right around the corner from my favourite store, Selfridges.

It seems like a place for people serious about wine. What is Laure Patry's area of expertise?
Laure is fantastic; I've never known anyone with such a passion for wine. She has had complete freedom with the wine list and while many of the top wine regions are showcased, the list also highlights many of the smaller growers who take a minimum intervention approach to wine making. The main focus is on boutique wineries. All our staff are also trained sommeliers, too.

Is there one thing you do particularly well there?
The idea is to have wines for every occasion. We also offer a great selection of port and sherries to complement many of the tapas dishes. We also have a retail area where you can buy much of the wine we sell on the menu, as well as Zalto glasses, wine books, decanters and wine accessories like Coravin.

What came first, the food or the wine?
Frankie Van Loo and I very much worked together on this. We started food tastings along with Laure back at the start of this year to ensure we were all reading off the same page and that everything married up as we had planned.

Why is there a growing interest in wine in London?
In London we can have easy access to any wine around the world, so that makes it interesting and also sets a

challenge as there is a large choice. I think people are much more aware and confident with wine now than they were, say, 10 years ago. Sommeliers have a big part to play in that as they constantly educate their guests and advise on how and why a particular wine works well with a dish. I think people want to learn.

Do you think that people are buying wine in a different way now?
I think people like to be guided and the sommelier is really the link between the producer and the guest. I think people are ready to spend more when they understand the quality of the wine they are getting.

Is the feel or design of a wine bar different to, say, a cocktail bar or restaurant?
Yes, there is the obvious functional difference, but I think a wine bar should be a little more plush. **VS**

Social Wine & Tapas 39 James Street W1U 1DL
020 7993 3257 socialwineandtapas.com

Other London wine bars:

10 Cases Covent Garden WC2

28–50 Wine Workshop & Kitchen Marylebone W1

40 Maltby Street Bermondsey SE1

Antidote Soho W1

Gordon's Charing Cross WC2

Mission Bethnal Green E2

The Remedy Fitzrovia W1

Sager + Wilde Haggerston E2

Terroir Covent Garden WC2

Vinoteca Various locations

MAYFAIR & SOHO

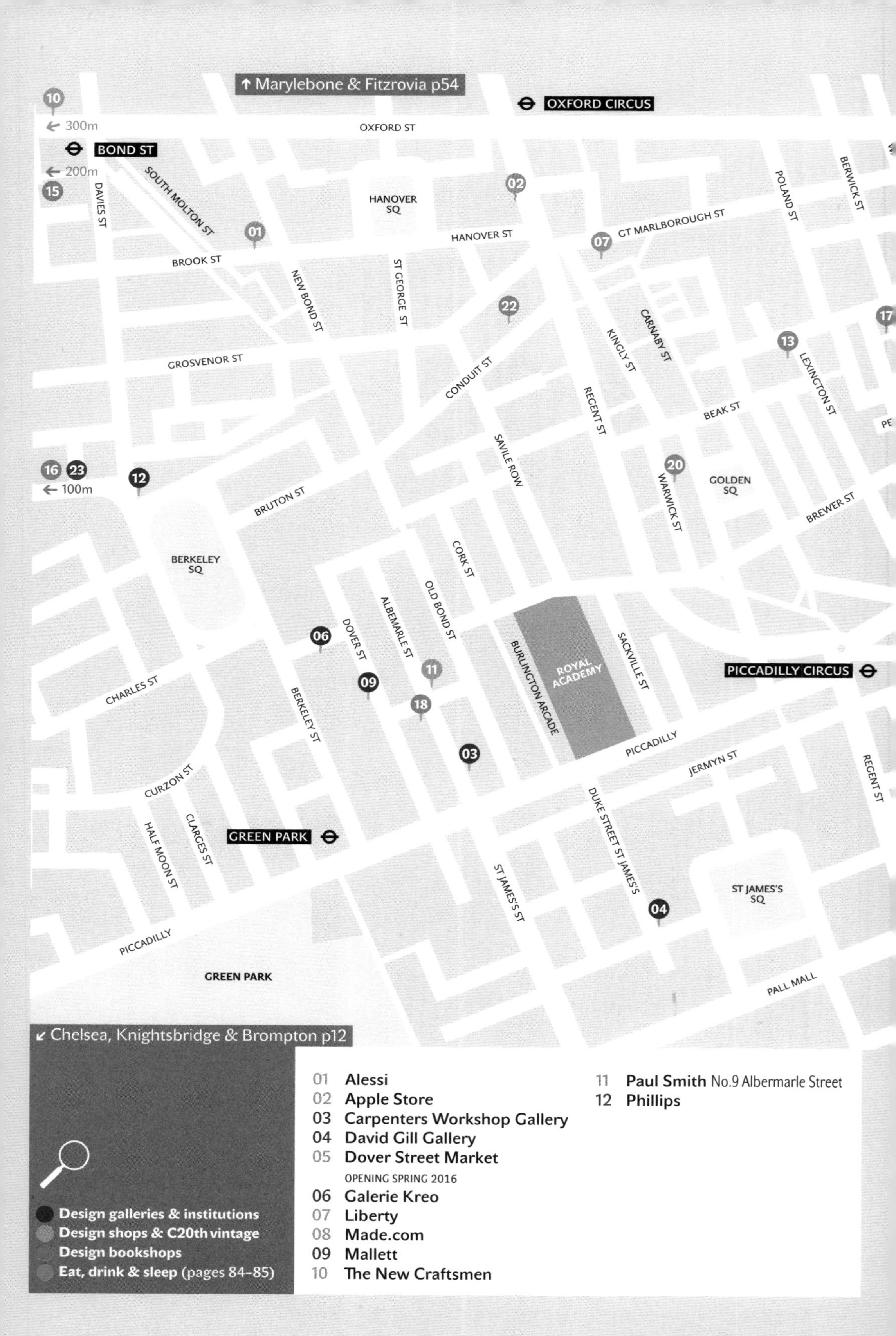
↑ Marylebone & Fitzrovia p54
OXFORD CIRCUS
OXFORD ST
BOND ST
← 300m
← 200m
← 100m
DAVIES ST
SOUTH MOLTON ST
BROOK ST
HANOVER SQ
HANOVER ST
NEW BOND ST
ST GEORGE ST
GT MARLBOROUGH ST
POLAND ST
BERWICK ST
CARNABY ST
KINGLY ST
GROSVENOR ST
CONDUIT ST
REGENT ST
LEXINGTON ST
BEAK ST
SAVILE ROW
WARWICK ST
GOLDEN SQ
BREWER ST
BRUTON ST
BERKELEY SQ
CORK ST
OLD BOND ST
ALBEMARLE ST
DOVER ST
BURLINGTON ARCADE
ROYAL ACADEMY
SACKVILLE ST
PICCADILLY CIRCUS
CHARLES ST
BERKELEY ST
PICCADILLY
JERMYN ST
CURZON ST
GREEN PARK
HALF MOON ST
CLARGES ST
DUKE STREET ST JAMES'S
ST JAMES'S ST
ST JAMES'S SQ
GREEN PARK
PALL MALL
↙ Chelsea, Knightsbridge & Brompton p12
Design galleries & institutions
Design shops & C20th vintage
Design bookshops
Eat, drink & sleep (pages 84–85)
01 Alessi
02 Apple Store
03 Carpenters Workshop Gallery
04 David Gill Gallery
05 Dover Street Market
OPENING SPRING 2016
06 Galerie Kreo
07 Liberty
08 Made.com
09 Mallett
10 The New Craftsmen
11 Paul Smith No.9 Albermarle Street
12 Phillips

Mayfair & Soho

The yin and yang of the West End, Mayfair and Soho have grown together in recent years. As real estate soars, Soho's less salubrious businesses shutter, Mayfair's Regency mansions open up to fashion brands and Regent Street, now smarter than ever, acts as a bridge. A foodie revolution has discerning diners exploring both sides. They've got plenty to feast their eyes on, design-wise. Among Mayfair's auction houses, fresh blood like The New Craftsmen and even Paul Smith exhibit approachable vintage and craft. Between them, the Apple Store is a reality check in the slick and ultra-modern.

01 **Alessi**
22 Brook Street W1K 5DF
020 7518 9091
alessi.com
Mon-Sat 10-6.30, Thu 10-7, Sun 12-6

This is the London flagship of the Italian utensil company that did some of its most iconic work in the 1980s. Pierre Charpin, Toyo Ito and Monica Förster have all helped keep the company relevant in the 21st century.

02 **Apple Store**
235 Regent Street W1B 2EL
020 7153 9000
apple.com
Mon-Sat 10-9, Sun 12-6

Here on Regent Street, and in the stores that have followed worldwide, Apple has designed one of the most successful face-to-face experiences in retail. There are few Grade II-listed buildings, in London or elsewhere, that can boast queues of tech-savvy youth waiting by the doors for the 10am opening. This could've been the kind of place to bring even informed consumers to tears, yet Apple staffers are helpful, experienced and honest. And they'll let you test the heck out of the equipment, even if they know you're bound to leave empty handed. This longtime Apple user was especially sceptical of the Genius Bar, a free service for customers having technical issues. But it's easy to get same-day service, provided you book online before opening hours. Can Dell say as much?

Makers and shakers

Catherine Lock, Natalie Melton & Mark Henderson, *The New Craftsmen*

Catherine Lock, Natalie Melton and Mark Henderson had worked in three distinct but overlapping metiers – sourcing and developing design; developing sponsorship and mentorship programmes; and managing luxury brands, respectively – when they met five years ago and resolved to collaborate. Through a series of pop-up shops and exhibitions under the name The New Craftsmen, they've nurtured and represented more than 75 British craftspeople. In 2014 they launched their first permanent showroom in a historic 185-square-metre space in a quiet corner of Mayfair.

How did you all come together?
Natalie: Mark and I met through a mentoring programme for craft-makers that I was organising called Crafted. Mark was one of the mentors.
Catherine: I'd been sourcing design in Asia for Sainsbury's and had been getting really down about the mass-market, homogenised high street. I was learning that people were willing to pay a little more for provenance behind things, to understand how they're made and connect with producers. After I left Sainsbury's I took myself on a trip to some very remote places in Britain that had a distinctive craft culture. When I came back I had a newfound knowledge of how things have grown from local needs.
Natalie: I knew that Mark's interest in craft extended beyond mentoring and I thought he'd be interested in meeting Catherine and hearing a bit about the road trip she'd done meeting craftspeople around Britain.
Mark: I'd been thinking, 'Craftsmen can't be all things to all people. They can't do trademarks, legal contracts, PR… why aren't people representing their work?' There was a lack of recognition of good craft and a lack of retail space for it. And knowing the luxury industry was becoming increasingly interested in bespoke and where things came from, we started drinking coffee and trying to work out whether this was doable.

Has craft become a luxury commodity?
Catherine: I'd say it's about customers' understanding of what they find. Understanding what you're buying is

03 Carpenters Workshop Gallery
3 Albemarle Street W1S 4HE
020 3051 5939
carpentersworkshopgallery.com
Mon-Fri 10-6

This is one of London's first forums for collectible design, and everything shown in the pared-back, slick-surfaced space can be classified as furniture: it should be used, albeit with care. Founders Loic Le Gaillard and Julien Lombrail have a singular eye for talent, and past contributors have included Maarten Baas, Atelier Van Lieshout, Marc Newson and Andrea Branzi.

04 David Gill Gallery
2-4 King Street SW1Y 6QP
020 3195 6600
davidgillgallery.com
Mon-Fri 10-6, Sat 11-6

David Gill is one of the reasons auction houses like Christie's have embraced design as a high-art form. The Spanish veteran cut his teeth showing Europeans like Eileen Gray and Charlotte Perriand in the 1980s before adopting indefatigable Brits like Ron Arad. He made stars of surrealist designers Fredrikson Stallard and was instrumental in adding 'furniture designer' to Zaha Hadid's repertoire.

05 Dover Street Market
18–21 Haymarket SW1Y 4DG
020 7518 0680
doverstreetmarket.com
Mon-Wed 11-6.30, Thu-Sat 11-7, Sun 12-5

At its core, Dover Street Market is a fashion retailer at the very cutting edge. The meticulous eye of Comme des Garçons' Rei Kawakubo governs a tightly curated selection of designer wear. Design and architecture lovers flock here for the clothing as well as the imaginative showspaces made from ramshackle materials against which the garments and accessories shine. The store is due to move from its original premises at 17–18 Dover Street to a much larger space in Haymarket in spring 2016.

a mindset that takes time, with knowledge built up over years. People who buy what we sell have already got that mindset and have made it a priority to purchase things that are more enduring and meaningful. That, to me, is the big difference between us and a luxury brand.

Do you sometimes feel like you've been instrumental in elevating craft?
Natalie: We feel like we captured the zeitgeist and did something with it. The mood music around craftsmanship has been building for a few years. I come from an art background and there was a frustration with the increasingly overblown, conceptual art that had very little beauty or substance. Now the art market is moving more toward what they'd term 'applied arts'. So it was a way of redressing the balance.

> **"This guy walked in the other day and gasped, 'It smells like my childhood.' Obviously something about it hit him in a really powerful way."**

Will craft become increasingly affordable now that there are more people selling and supporting it?
Natalie: Nobody ever asks if art is too expensive. If it's something you really value and appreciate and get a lot of emotional sustenance from...
Catherine: There should be no difference between the bowl that stands on your table and one you put on the wall.

Tell me about your Mayfair space.
Mark: When we looked at it, it was horrible, but the building is beautiful – an 1895 breeches factory. We were able to strip it back to its barest essentials, and it's got wonderful light. We're just 100 yards from Selfridges, so in terms of accessibility, it's a great location.

What sort of response do your customers generally have to the space?
Natalie: They have a very emotional reaction. This guy walked in the other day and gasped, 'It smells like my childhood.' Obviously something about it hit him in a really powerful way. He got quite choked up. It's definitely a step outside hectic life, and the objects you take away become talismans of that, to remind you of a different way of being. It's food for the soul.
Catherine: Craft purchases are much more emotional. People really engage with the space. It feels completely different from hectic Oxford Street. They walk in here and physically sigh with relief. That was purposeful. We wanted to make it a more human kind of place.

Tell me about some of the traditional skills that you've helped to revive.
Natalie: Swill basket-making is a traditional method that uses cleft oak. There are only four swillers left in the country and one is a young woman called Lorna Singleton. She paired up with Sebastian Cox and made the Scorched Shake Sideboard.

What's your recruiting process like?
Mark: When we did our first pop-up, we drew up a list of 32 people that we wanted to work with. Since then, it's been about personal recommendation from makers and people coming to us.

Is there anyone that you would say completely embodies what you would like to represent?
Mark: Gareth Neal is truly a master of what he does. He's also evangelical about it. His Brodgar chair, made with the Orkney chair-maker Kevin Gauld, is our iconic product, a beautiful piece that fits comfortably into a contemporary environment.
Natalie: Catarina Riccabona, a hand-weaver, was making scarves and cushions to sell at open studios when we met her. We opened up a network of interior designers for her, which means increasingly she's being commissioned to make more ambitious pieces of work.

How have you, personally, changed your habits or your homes over your time working with craft?
Catherine: Hand on heart, I can say I've completely changed. Whenever I can, I save up and I know I'm going to be getting something I truly love, not only because it's beautiful, but whenever I use it I remember I've engaged an individual to make it for me – and it's benefitting that individual. I have a bowl from a slipware potter I bought on my journey around the country. I can't not use it in the morning.
Mark: I would like to start again. I'm saving up. EH

10 **The New Craftsmen**
34 North Row W1K 6DG (See page 81)

Hammer time
Alexander Payne, *Phillips*

Twentieth-century applied arts and design have been popular with collectors for some time and works from past masters such as Jean Prouvé, Gio Ponti, Poul Henningsen, Jean Royère, Jean-Michel Frank, Charlotte Perriand and Le Corbusier sell at impressive prices at auction. In recent years, works by living designers including Zaha Hadid, Nendo and Studio Job have been fetching surprising amounts under the hammer, illustrating a growing appetite from collectors for the cutting edge. Alexander Payne is in charge of hunting down these functional and conceptual treasures at the international auction house Phillips.

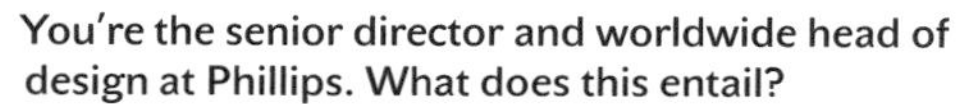

You're the senior director and worldwide head of design at Phillips. What does this entail?
I head up the international design team at Phillips and am responsible for working with our global specialists to consign and sell works in our design auctions. The design department at Phillips has a reputation of delivering carefully edited, museum-quality sales. We have a meticulous and highly curatorial approach to delivering work to the design market, showcasing and presenting the world's leading designers.

What are some of the challenges in tracking down truly credible items for auction?
The biggest challenge is finding works with exceptional provenance that are museum quality, as well as being fresh and exciting to our existing international buyers while also being attractive to new collectors.

What are the preferences of today's collectors?
The market is very interested in understanding the roots and origins of design. Collectors continue to look at the entire 20th and 21st centuries for masterpieces throughout this more-than-100-year range.

What are some of the greatest shifts you've seen in the time you've been working at Phillips?
The broadening of the market for collectors is one of the most interesting shifts. We have also witnessed the inception of highly established markets such as Nordic design, ceramics, Italian glass and French midcentury design. Collectors are seeking works in all fields and also continue to look back to the art deco period.

How does design collecting compare to the lofty heights of art collecting?
Today we see more and more collectors of 20th-century and contemporary art shifting towards collecting 20th-century decorative arts and design. The collectors appreciate the importance of collecting across all modern and contemporary cultures.

Is there an item you've tracked down that you're particularly proud of, or one that you personally love?
We were humbled to be able to offer the Isamu Noguchi Conger Goodyear table at auction in December 2014. This imposing sculptural icon, designed for the then-president of the Museum of Modern Art, is widely

considered one of the most important American design works of the 20th century. Our clients were overjoyed to be able to see this masterpiece in the flesh, which before then had enjoyed a mythological status in the design community. We were also extremely fortunate to be able to include the Lockheed Lounge by Marc Newson in our design auction in April 2015. There are only 15 examples of this lounge in existence and four of these are in museum collections. Thanks to the combined expertise and knowledge of our international design team, we set the world record for Marc Newson, yet again, with its sale. **MF**

12 Phillips 30 Berkeley Square W1J 6EX
(See page 81)

Other leading auction houses for 20th and 21st century design:

Bonhams
101 New Bond Street W1S 1SR
bonhams.com

Christie's
8 King Street SW1Y 6QT
christies.com

Sotheby's
34–35 New Bond Street W1A 2AA
sothebys.com

Galerie Kreo juxtaposes old with new in its Mayfair space

06 Galerie Kreo
14A Hay Hill W1J 8NZ
020 7499 4611
galeriekreo.fr
Tues-Sat 10-6

This the new London outpost of the hip design gallery that has been supplying Paris with collectible design since 1999. Owners Didier and Clemence Krzentowski are collectors to be reckoned with, boasting the world's largest collection of Gino Sarfatti lights and a shocking stockpile of Castiglioni, Paulin and Pierre Guariche furniture. In 2014 they opened their slim London gallery (Esperanto for 'creation') to service like-minded collectors here and be closer to talents like Doshi Levien and Jasper Morrison. Meanwhile, they put their creative welly behind playful exhibitions featuring vintage Sarfatti and brand new Jaime Hayon. It's a heavyweight diversion in a corner of Mayfair that can get a bit full of itself.

07 Liberty
Regent Street W1B 5AH
020 7734 1234
liberty.co.uk
Mon-Sat 10-8, Sun 12-6

This retrograde Tudor revival building, built around a wonderful central atrium and dotted with discreet staircases, still stocks the conservative cotton florals, Indian baby chairs and vintage pantry cupboards that it made its name with, but now offers contemporary wares from the likes of Case, Vitra, Tom Dixon, De Padova, Hay and Re-Found Objects.

08 Made.com
100 Charing Cross Road
WC2H 0JG
made.com
Mon-Sat 10-8, Sun 12-6

Made is the young online made-to-order furniture biz that passes on savings from its no-warehouse, no-middle man approach to retail. For those who need to try before they buy, this large showroom is the central London convenience point. Whatever is on display is featured on the website, so check in advance. Otherwise, tip up for hands-on advice on the hundreds of affordable, if somewhat derivative, furniture and lighting options.

09 Mallett
Ely House, 37 Dover Street
W1S 4NJ
020 7499 7411
mallettantiques.com
Mon–Fri 10–6

You might be surprised to find one of London's oldest established antique dealers in this guide. However, as well as being a specialist in the finest furniture, art, clocks and objets d'art, it also focuses on the contemporary through its sister company, Meta. It commissions pieces designed by the likes of Tord Boontje, Barber Osgerby, Matali Crasset and Klauser and Carpenter, fabricated by Europe's finest master craftsmen. Juxtaposing old with new, the exquisite changing displays are housed within the magnificent neoclassical Ely House, originally built as a London base for the Bishop of Ely in 1772.

10 The New Craftsmen
34 North Row W1K 6DG
020 7148 3190
thenewcraftsmen.com
Mon–Sat 10–6

Visitors breathe a collective sigh of relief when they enter, and it's no wonder. The New Craftsmen is barely 30m from one of the city's most chaotic corners, but it's like stepping into a simpler era. Everything in the whitewashed space has been handcrafted, hand-knitted, hand-turned in the UK – sometimes over days of slow, methodical work. The owners, three entrepreneurs devoted to raising the profile of traditional craft and its practitioners, work in the back along with a handful of employees, so there's always someone in house to tell the spirited stories behind each piece. The only downside is having to go back out into the trenches. (See pages 74–77)

11 Paul Smith No.9 Albermarle Street
9 Albemarle Street W1S 4BL
020 7493 4565
paulsmith.co.uk
Mon–Wed 10–6, Thu–Sat 10–7, Sun 12–6

When it comes to his stores, leading British fashion designer Paul Smith doesn't opt for an identikit global identity. Instead, he favours diversity, eclecticism and fun. Different from the clothing focus of his other stores, this Mayfair flagship is also a sort of playground for his lifelong obsession with collecting bits and bobs from around the world. Lovingly restored furniture sits alongside artworks, objects and curiosities touched by the designer himself. And best of all, they're all for sale, making the space an evolving proposition on each visit.

12 Phillips
30 Berkeley Square W1J 6EX
020 7318 4010
phillips.com
When on view: Mon–Sat 10–6, Sun 12–6

Standing proud on Berkeley Square, global auction house Phillips seems intimidating, but the security guards are there to watch over the contemporary art, photography and design – not to put you off. Design exhibitions are staged twice a year, a bonanza of Ponti, Prouvé and Kjaerholm, plus some contemporary stars. Views from the seventh floor are spectacular. (See pages 78–79)

SOHO
CREATE
FESTIVAL
SOHO
CREATE
3 – 7 JUNE 2015
BUY TICKETS NOW
sohocreate.co.uk
BT
NEXT GEN
Shaftesbury
SOHO ESTATES
SOHO THEATRE
City of Westminster
QUEENS
THEATRE
GIELGU
BELLA
ITALIA
Les Misérables
LYRIC
KRISTIN
SCOTT
THOMAS
THE AUDIENCE
THRILLER
Euro World
Currency
Bureau de Change
THE WORLD'S LONGES

Stage presence
Tom Harvey
SohoCreate festival

Behind Soho's bustling street life and thriving entertainment scene are offices and studios full of creative businesses and highly skilled talent. In 2014, Tom Harvey founded SohoCreate, an annual celebration of this creative prowess and a platform for discussion on the very subject of creativity. Over three days in June, Soho becomes the stage for a wide cross-section of individuals to meet and talk about what they do and why they do it.

What was your motivation for launching SohoCreate?
I grew up in a creative family, always doing creative things, so I'm relaxed with creativity. I found myself at conferences, supposedly about creativity but usually a bloke talking earnestly about his own brilliance.

Talking with creative people, I found they were bored of having to hard-sell in a noisy world. They wanted more meaningful conversations about why and how they do what they do. They wanted a festival on their doorstep that championed London's creativity, giving everyone a chance to talk in more depth about creativity itself.

I was astounded to find how the creative sector in Soho had grown. It's no longer just the film and SFX sectors. It's now made up of design, architecture, fashion, theatre, music and restaurants – clearly a phenomenal creative cluster. In 2014, we staged an early version of the festival and it attracted about 1,000 people. And, in 2015, about double that attended the talks, creative open house events, exhibitions, workshops and screenings. We closed Greek Street and Frith Street to create a party atmosphere. It's now a full-on strategy to build a huge creative festival for London.

At SohoCreate, you describe Soho as "the world's most creative square mile". Can you explain why?
Westminster City Council was the first investor in SohoCreate. They are quite rightly very keen on an evidence base to inform their investment strategy. We did an analysis of the Soho cluster to better understand it. What came back was astounding – 46,000 creative workers, turning over £7.5billion, hundreds of international awards, 10,000 new jobs in the past five years and 20 per cent of London's new creative jobs. The Soho Cluster contains 11 per cent of the creative industry turnover of the entire country. That density of creativity is unrivalled anywhere in the world, so it was a short step to saying with confidence that it is the most creative square mile in the world.

Presumably there is a lot of competition within this concentrated area?
Soho is not a place to be half-hearted. It houses some of the best creative talent in the world, so your ideas have to be good, just to get through the day. I love that creative pressure, that appetite for real quality; it forces you to be at your best. It also means that you can build very high-quality collaborations with brilliant people just around the corner.

Some people bemoan the gentrification of Soho. What do you make of this change?
I don't find gentrification to be a useful word. It implies the deliberate development or regeneration of an area for the rich or elite. Most creative people are neither, and for the most part they are the occupiers of Soho. There is something more complicated going on. Central London is evolving, rapidly. Nothing stays the same, nor should it. I have no patience with those who want to keep Soho as it was. What they mean is that they want the places they like and frequent to stay unchanged. That isn't an option in a modern city. **MF**

SohoCreate takes place across Soho in June
sohocreate.co.uk

For snacks/dinner
13 Bao
53 Lexington Street W1F 9AS
baolondon.com

Primarily a bun bar run by three former street food-trading friends with design degrees, it offers illustrated menus, pretty homemade Taiwanese bao buns and pig's blood cake.

For quiet coffee
14 Bar Termini
7 Old Compton Street W1D 5JE
07860 945018
bar-termini.com

A small and sophisticated coffee bar from London's cocktail maestro Tony Conigliaro.

For dinner
15 The Colony Grill
The Beaumont
8 Balderton Street W1K 6TN
020 7499 9499
colonygrillroom.com

The Beaumont hotel's luscious, red-leather Transatlantic restaurant features hints from other restaurants in the Corbin & King stable. Come for Kenny's meatloaf on Mondays.

For cocktails
16 The Connaught Bar
Carlos Place W1K 2AL
020 7499 7070
the-connaught.co.uk

This is an excellent space for first dates, with its high ceilings, glass and mirror work, stunning deep red and black leather couches, and world class bar team. Just make sure you dress up.

For beer
17 Duck & Rice
90 Berwick Street W1F 0QB
020 3327 7888
theduckandrice.com

Wagamama king Alan Yau's new pub has a large range of tank beers, glaringly shiny fittings and lots of metal and mirrors. The restaurant upstairs offers a Chinese menu. You'll need to book ahead.

For a spicy lunch
18 Gymkhana
42 Albemarle Street W1S 4JH
020 3011 5900
gymkhanalondon.com

The brooding rattan and dark wood-panelled interior matches the rich, authentic dishes of this Michelin-starred Indian kitchen run by Karam Sethi.

For a Japanese breakfast
19 Koya Bar
49 Frith Street W1D 4SG
020 7433 4463
koya.co.uk

Cute Japanese bar serving bowls of excellent okayu (rice porridge) and udon noodles for breakfast on beautiful crockery.

For a Middle Eastern breakfast
20 Nopi
21–22 Warwick Street W1B 5NE
020 7494 9584
ottolenghi.co.uk/locations

Elegant marble and brass restaurant run by London's

Left, Koya Bar is the place for oodles of silky smooth noodles

Above, dusty pink dining at Sketch's Gallery restaurant

Eat, drink & sleep

sophisticated salad king, Yotam Ottolenghi. Start the day with the brightening shakshuka made with smoked labneh.

For a punchy dinner
21 The Palomar
34 Rupert Street W1D 6DN
020 7439 8777
thepalomar.co.uk

This much lauded restaurant serves "josperised" dishes from deconstructed kebabs to octo-hummus cooked by excitable chefs who sing as they cook.

For fantastical drinks
22 Sketch
9 Conduit Street W1S 2XG
020 7659 4500
sketch.london

Drinking in The Glade is akin to being in a tropical Rococo painting – but with better cocktails. Watch your bill, mind, as these ain't cheap. And check out the infamous toilets.

BOOK A ROOM

For classic meets contemporary
23 The Connaught
Carlos Place W1K 2AL
020 7499 7070
the-connaught.co.uk

For Georgian-style comfort
24 Dean Street Townhouse
69–71 Dean Street W1D 3SE
020 7434 1775
deanstreettownhouse.com

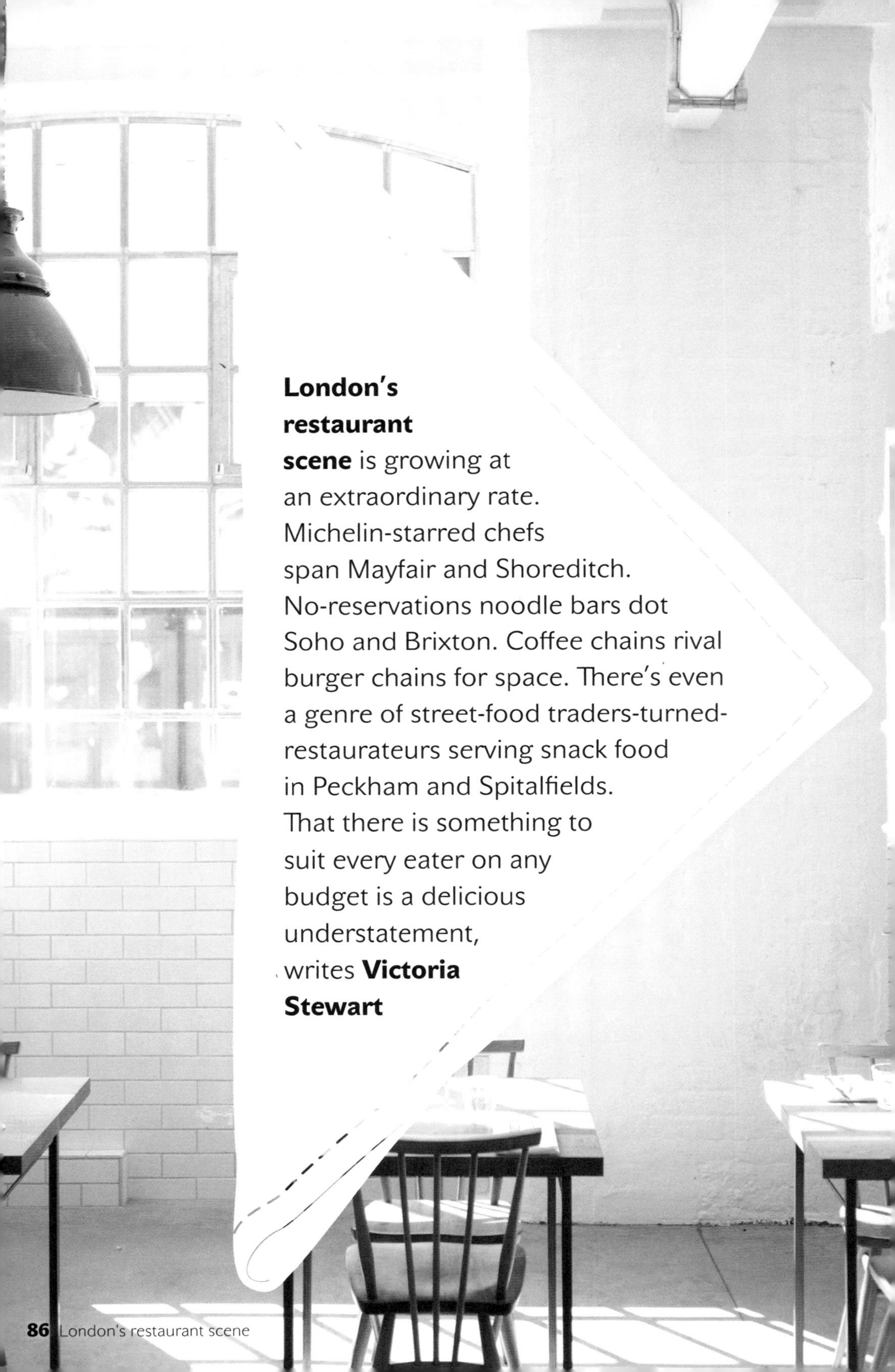

London's restaurant scene is growing at an extraordinary rate. Michelin-starred chefs span Mayfair and Shoreditch. No-reservations noodle bars dot Soho and Brixton. Coffee chains rival burger chains for space. There's even a genre of street-food traders-turned-restaurateurs serving snack food in Peckham and Spitalfields. That there is something to suit every eater on any budget is a delicious understatement, writes **Victoria Stewart**

Naturally, the accompanying news feed never sleeps. Hungry punters, keen to know where to find their next fix, need only subscribe to online publications issuing monthly lists of the best restaurant openings or newsletters sent from restaurant website Hot Dinners to tens of thousands of diners, or to seek out devoted food photo sharers on social media, which is still widely influencing our eating habits.

Today, design and branding – everything from light fixtures to menus, uniforms and paintwork – has played an integral role in our experience of eating out. Indeed, while these might take two years' planning, a fit-out might only take a matter of days – and this is now as scrutinised as the food itself.

Fitting roughly into three categories, there are places that expound the clean, reflective, utilitarian look that started at St John and has been taken in various guises to Hereford Road, Dabbous, Portland and, to some extent, the minimalist Bao. Secondly, there is a band of traditional, comfortable and opulent dining rooms. At Dinner by Heston Blumenthal, where the menu is based around Tudor feasting food, chefs can be watched inside a great glass box and lights have been designed using original Hampton Court Palace Tudor jelly moulds. Perhaps the most widely recognised design choice, obvious at Polpo, 40 Maltby Street and Primeur, is shabby chic, invariably a combination of exposed brick, filament bulbs, and upcycled or distressed furniture.

But today what defines London's restaurants at nearly every level is their understanding and promotion of native British ingredients. James Lowe's talent at Lyle's is in being able to source the most flavoursome, serving them simply but not unskilfully. At Smoking Goat, chefs use wild British herbs to make Thai salads, and London-based Cobble Lane Cured produces cured British meats for Smokehouse and Jamie Oliver's Barbacoa restaurants. It has taken time for this feeding frenzy to develop. The 2015 publication of *Harden's London Restaurants* featured 148 restaurant launches; while one might expect to see an equal number of closures, they were actually at their lowest point since 2000. So how has it come about?

Lyle's restaurant, Shoreditch

Left to right, Bao, Soho; The Clove Club, Shoreditch; Primeur, Islington (above); Polpo, Soho (below)

In 2008 the recession stirred up London's dining out scene. Some who had previously never considered careers in hospitality found themselves without jobs – but with time to scope out the industry. It also bred the kind of risk-taking attitude that comes out of a period of financial uncertainty, which in this case manifested itself in several exciting food ventures, from street food vans to pop-up events. Some of these have turned into London's biggest restaurant success stories, notably the Meatliquor burger brigade and the Pizza Pilgrims duo.

Often the personal nature of these is communicated either through vibrant signage or a conversation had with the person making the foods. Let's take Mark Edwards, who, having been made redundant from his job at a freight forwarding company, set up his idea for an Austrian food stall, FleischMob, which he now runs in the form of stalls and kitchen residencies. These he furnishes simply with red and white checked tablecloths, menus featuring a mixture of olde Austrian bierhaus and punky fonts, and an illustrated backdrop of the London skyline blended with snowy mountains.

Also around this time a new class of chef began to spring up; one who respected staff and could thus run more agreeable kitchens, which in turn affected the sort of food and service created from them. Those who have worked under tough management are now running superb open, friendlier kitchens, which set the tone for much of a restaurant's identity, for example at The Clove Club or The Kitchen Table.

Here food is bright and uninhibited, menus are concise and cleanly designed, interiors are stripped-back but inviting and staff might be dressed in jeans and collarless denim shirts. Meanwhile, there is music during prep time – Ollie Dabbous of the eponymous restaurant in Fitzrovia listens to Dr John as he prepares his Michelin-starred plates.

Travel, too, has led to interesting influences from countries in South East Asia and the Middle East, while increasing numbers of travellers to New York have brought ideas back. With this access we have seen cunning restaurateurs like Russell Norman and Richard Beatty set up

their ever-widening stable of Polpo restaurants – created with Italian bacari and New York speakeasies in mind. Or near Liverpool Street is the expandable HOP takeaway Vietnamese concept, thought up by former City worker Paul Hopper, who quit his job as an M&A analyst at Investec to spend six months travelling around Vietnam.

International interest in London as a place to import fast-casual food businesses is illustrated by a rush of chains, from the American burrito giant Chipotle in 2011 – there are now six – or in 2013 the arrival of the burger diners, Shake Shack and Five Guys, or indeed the London outpost of Keith McNally's Balthazar from New York.

So this is the decade of London foodism. But the question now is: does its thriving market have space for more?

Well, it is a tough industry to crack. There are those who have failed – brash restaurateurs driven by trendy concepts rather than business sense; those with effective ideas but no grasp of marketing; others whose kitchens or surroundings are not up to scratch.

The success of restaurants in active, exciting market areas such as Soho and Shoreditch, and increasingly Brixton, has much to do with the fact that smaller, modestly designed spaces mean relatively affordable rents; yet this is now being challenged by the threat of greedy landlords citywide. Islington's Upper Street, for example, is fast being filled with businesses with much deeper pockets.

But there are still small fish to fry. In Old Spitalfields Market there is a push to welcome back independent business – Blixen restaurant has arrived from the owners of the Riding House Café – or in Peckham where pop-ups like Forza Win or charmingly pared-back start-ups like Miss Tapas are quickly securing local fan bases.

From its food to the accompanying service and settings, the best bits of London's restaurant scene are currently characterised by an attention to detail and British produce, creativity and an easy-going self-confidence. We must work hard not to let those standards slip.

Opposite left to right, Hoi Polloi, Shoreditch (above); Blixen, Spitalfields (below); Blixen, Spitalfields; Dinner by Heston Blumenthal, Knightsbridge

Victoria Stewart is a London-based freelance food and travel writer who writes for *standard.co.uk*, *ES Magazine*, *The Sunday Telegraph* and *Unmapped*

COVENT GARDEN & HOLBORN

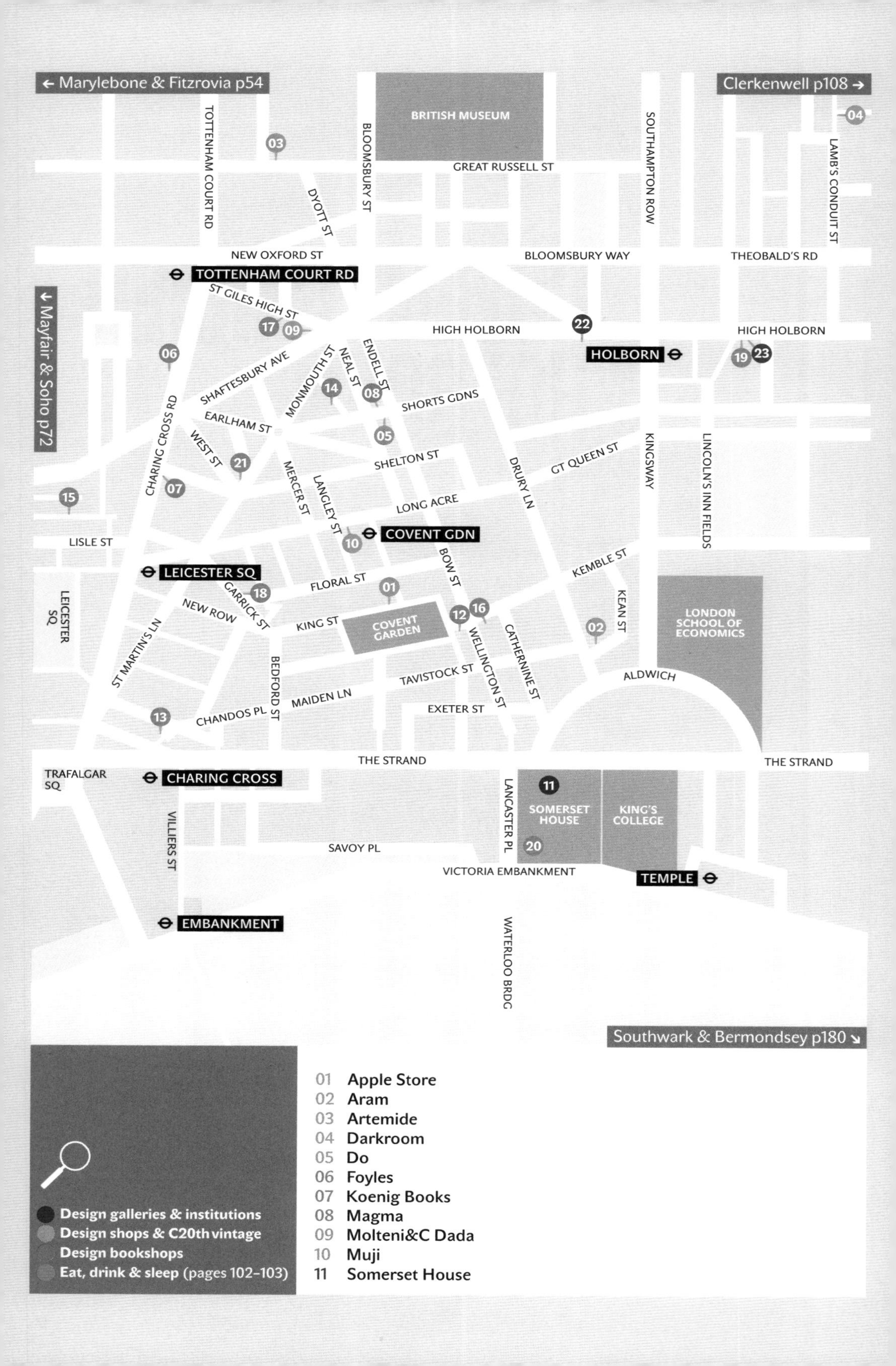

01 Apple Store
02 Aram
03 Artemide
04 Darkroom
05 Do
06 Foyles
07 Koenig Books
08 Magma
09 Molteni&C Dada
10 Muji
11 Somerset House

Covent Garden & Holborn

Theatreland isn't all dash and flash – though you won't believe it standing outside the Apple Store in Covent Garden. Beyond the market are quiet spaces to explore, from the creative hub Somerset House to the off-piste streets of Bloomsbury (Lamb's Conduit Street remains one of London's great independent routes). Charing Cross has lost its more eccentric bookshops but those remaining are more edifying than ever. The tangle of streets in Covent Garden will never make navigating easy, but the opening of Crossrail in 2018 should at least make them more accessible.

01 Apple Store
1–7 The Piazza WC2E 8HA
020 7447 1400
apple.com
Mon–Sat 10–9, Sun 12–6

Apple has done right by this 150-year-old, Grade II-listed building, enlisting Bohlin Cywinski Jackson architects to restore the outdoor colonnade, interior brick walls and exquisite iron arches, while also adding a multi-faceted skylight, creating a dazzling atrium. Apple also appears to have thrown more brainpower at this Genius Bar than at other locations.

02 Aram
110 Drury Lane WC2B 5SG
020 7557 7557
aram.co.uk
Mon–Sat 10–6 Thurs 10–7

Aram has been synonymous with contemporary lifestyle since before there was such a thing. It took Zeev Aram to convince London there was a modern alternative to Chippendale. His first space on the King's Road, acquired in the mid-1960s, distributed designs by Le Corbusier, Perriand and Castiglioni that were so foreign to these parts as to be shocking. The 1,800-square-metre industrial space at Drury Lane is run by an effortlessly knowledgeable team, who pay as much heed to those designers as manufacturers like Tecta and Arper. (See pages 94–97)

03 Artemide
106 Great Russell Street WC1B 3NB
020 7291 3853
artemide.com
Mon–Sat 9–5 (closed for lunch 1–1.30)

Artemide has been in the business of simple, bare-bones lighting since 1960, providing not only wow-factor installations for retailers and hoteliers, but also home lighting solutions that could well change your life. The latter is what this boutique, housed in a Bloomsbury townhouse just off Tottenham Court Road, is all about.

04 Darkroom
52 Lamb's Conduit Street WC1N 3LL
020 7831 7244
darkroomlondon.com
Mon–Fri 11–7, Sat 11–6,
Sun & bank holidays 12–5

Art is design, design is fashion and fashion is art in this boutique that defies categorisation but which stands out for its futuristic directional feel, thanks to the vision of founders Rhonda Drakeford and Lulu Roper-Caldbeck, providing the browser with a shopping experience free of gender stereotypes and traditional 'departments'.

05 Do
34 Shorts Gardens WC2H 9PX
020 7836 4039
do-shop.com
Mon–Sat 10–6.30, Thurs 10–8, Sun 12–6

Space comes at a premium in Covent Garden, which is why this oasis of top-notch design makes do with a glorified closet. Accessories come before furniture, but they're the kind of accessories that will make your life just as pleasurable as a sofa – like eccentric kitchen gadgets and storage solutions you didn't think you needed.

06 Foyles
107 Charing Cross Road WC2H 0DT
020 7434 1574
foyles.co.uk
Mon–Sat 9.30–9, Sun 11.30–6

Foyles has always been worth stopping in for a wander, but in 2014, the century-old bookseller relaunched in an airy, navigable flagship by Lifschutz Davidson Sandilands with a vast atrium and sweeping staircase to the incomparable cache of titles. If you visited in the opening week, you might have caught Michael Palin nip in to cut the ribbon

Design pioneer
Zeev Aram, *Aram*

The London design landscape was unimaginable 50 years ago. Before Zeev Aram opened his experimental space on the King's Road in 1964, good taste meant Chippendale and chintz, Eames was virtually unknown and a Wishbone was something you snapped at Christmas. Aram exposed Londoners to the Castiglioni brothers and Tobia Scarpa at their peak, becoming a retail giant and inspiring generations of like-minded entrepreneurs. In 1973 he moved into a multi-level space in Covent Garden and, in 2001, launched The Aram Gallery, showing radical, investigative design by industry upstarts. This year he unveiled a contract department on the lower-ground floor of the Drury Lane shop. We caught up with him there.

What prompted your interest in contemporary design?
I'd been in the navy and decided to change careers to architecture, but studying to be an architect took too long, so I came to London to design interiors for architects. That's when I developed an appreciation for modern European design. The lack of good, modern design here was disappointing. So after three years I decided to open my own practice. I thought, "If we're going to design interiors, I'll open a showroom for my clients." My lawyer asked me, "What are you going to sell?" I said, "I'll find something. And if not, I'll design something myself."

What did you end up selling?
In 1964 I went to Cologne, ran around like mad for three days and found nothing. Then I went to Milan and spoke to Dino Gavina to get the licence for Marcel Breuer's Wassily chair, and that was a revelation. I had never been to a business meeting and then suddenly we were negotiating over a bottle of whiskey. Through Gavina I got to know Tobia Scarpa, Vico Magistretti, and the Castiglionis. Those first weeks I would sit across the street at Alvaro's restaurant and watch people walking by. I didn't care if they hated it, I just didn't want them to ignore it. Or look but not see. I got some hate mail, and that was nice – any reaction was good. One of the first days, the photographer Claude Virgin was already waiting outside when I opened. He bought a Wassily chair for £49 10s and I watched him carry it home over his head, this big, burly man.

You've also sold your own designs and those of younger, up-and-coming designers. How has that mix changed over the years?
It hasn't changed. It's evolved. In the beginning I said if the business didn't work out, I'd sell my own stuff, but things got better. My Hockney table [the Altra table, immortalised in an oil painting by David Hockney] was successful because you could have a low version, a high one, wood, glass... And we did an interesting storage unit that Jasper Morrison redesigned and simplified. We're always searching for fresh blood.

Which of the younger talents are you most fond of?
There's Thomas Heatherwick. Konstantin Grcic – I like his lateral thinking. Martino Gamper – he goes off the beaten path. Jake Dyson is someone to watch: when we designed our new contract department, we used his lighting system.

You were once London's only purveyor of modern furniture. Now there's competition everywhere. What keeps you afloat?
You have to have principles, a certain attitude and appreciation. If you want to improve, you have to relinquish the rule that you have to be commercial, always selling. One of my rules is: if it's good looking and does what I want it to do, I'll sell it. Why change for the sake of changing? That's what I'm trying to instil in my daughter [Ruth], who's my buyer, and my son [Daniel], who's the managing director. The biggest compliment

I ever got was from somebody who was going to buy furniture for their children. They told them first to come by here to get the visual information and cultivate a taste.

Your gallery on the third floor is good for that: cultivating a taste.
It informs people using experimental design. Young designers show products that aren't even finished. Good designers still want to work with their hands, and that's what we show. Sometimes I watch the visitors smile, and that smile, for me, is worth everything. The gallery is my great interest. I do it for the industry.

How so?
There's no manufacturing in this country of any quality. We produce world-class designers, export them to Switzerland, Germany, Spain, then import their products. It's absurd. Now I have the space to invite industrialists to see what we can do. That will be my legacy: cultivating design and manufacturing in Britain. Our manufacturing is still in the hands of small makers - green shoots. Let's hope they turn into big oak trees.

You've been in Covent Garden for decades. Do you feel part of the fabric of the neighbourhood?
To me, Covent Garden has been ruined by its success. **EH**

02 Aram 110 Drury Lane WC2B 5SG (See page 93)

on the Travel section. These days you'll find the UK's largest foreign-language selection and a cracking magazine rack.

07 Koenig Books

80 Charing Cross Road WC2H 0BB
020 7240 8190
Mon-Fri 11-8, Sat 10-8

Koenig opened on Bookshop Row after enjoying huge success at the Serpentine Gallery. It doesn't see huge crowds, but it doesn't have downtime either; even mid-morning is a popular hour for flicking through a hefty tome dedicated to art, design, architecture, fashion and the like.

08 Magma

29 Shorts Gardens WC2H 9AP
020 7240 7970
magmabooks.com
Mon-Sat 11-7, Sun 12-6

It's been a pleasure to watch Magma, purveyor of arty books, magazines, prints and miscellany, expand from its first location down the road to this Shorts Gardens branch. It's also a pleasure to report that the place hasn't grown up too much. It still does guilty-pleasure typography tomes and pictogram T-shirts, and a kids' section that blends in with the adults because the toys appeal to everyone. Since the city has fallen for graphic design, Magma seems much less niche and more accessible to anyone in search of a unique gift. And if you're looking for the graphic novel which that geeky guy from your printmaking class recently put out on an obscure imprint, they'll likely have that too.

09 Molteni&C Dada

199 Shaftesbury Avenue WC2H 8JR
020 7631 2345
molteni.it
Mon- Fri 9-5.30, Thurs 9-8, Sat 10-4.30

Molteni took over this 400-square-metre space eight years ago from area veteran Christopher Wray for its Covent Garden flagship and replaced the obstacle course of pendant lights with the expansive wall systems and sectional sofas the brand is known for. A Molteni piece is an investment in time, space and money, as the staff here are aware, as they pay you the proper attention as you question the configurations of a mile-long floating desk by Rodolfo Dordoni. Italian kitchen brand Dada shares this sterling space.

10 Muji

37-38 Long Acre WC2E 9JT
020 7379 0820
muji.eu
Mon-Sat 10-8, Sun 12-6

The Muji name, so beloved by every class of consumer, has come to symbolise fuss-free merchandise in clean, efficient materials: stainless steel for kitchenware, porcelain for bathware, plastic for officeware and storage, and wood for furnishings. There are currently a dozen Muji locations across London. You'll never regret a visit to one of them and nearly always emerge with a problem solved.

11 Somerset House

Strand WC2R 1LA
020 7845 4600
somersethouse.org.uk
Daily 10-6

The allure was once purely seasonal: outdoor cinema in summer, ice skating in winter, Fashion Week in autumn… but now Somerset House has found its groove as an all-round culture destination. From the foyer behind the lavish renaissance courtyard, traffic flows in all directions. The East Wing, for dawdlers, has the magnificent Rizzoli bookshop; to the south are august galleries and the riverfront terrace, occupied by the successful Tom's Kitchen restaurants. Along the western flank are banks of new designer studios and, near the magnificent Spring restaurant, the Unseen Emporium, where alchemists, coders and anatomists display wearable technology with gothic, Victorian sensibility. (See pages 100–101)

Left, the latest location for Magma, purveyor of design books

Creative instigator
Jonathan Reekie, *Somerset House*

A renaissance is afoot at Somerset House, the neoclassical palace on the banks of the Thames. Mostly inhabited by functionaries since the 18th century, it recently saw out the Inland Revenue and saw in an army of creative tenants, including the resident creative workshop Makerversity. With the recent departure of Fashion Week, Somerset House has signed on as a central hub for the London Design Festival. That's due in no small part to the vision of incoming director Jonathan Reekie.

Somerset House used to seem a bit ominous to an outsider – a mammoth historic building without a coherent identity. How has that changed recently?
When the job came up, it really intrigued me because I thought, 'Great things happen there, but I can't quite figure out what it is.' There's been a huge amount of development, and the building work is done now. In some ways it's a start-up – if one with a great reputation, a strong brand, and a momentum and energy about it. So I feel I'm arriving at a perfect time to take stock and focus on Somerset House's core purpose.

Is that purpose to be a centre for British design?
I see Somerset House as being a centre for contemporary culture – but a different kind of centre. We've got the biggest community of creative businesses in London. What had been missing were artists and makers. As I was coming in, Makerversity had just arrived and was a key part of what I wanted to do, so that was serendipitous. The old ideas of art form and genre have begun to dissolve. I see Somerset House as a blank canvas that isn't tied down by its history. It will be much more porous, where artists can explore their practice, and audiences can encounter not just finished work but the process itself and the people who make it. I want us to be the R&D lab, factory and shop window all rolled into one.

Will you play a part in the London Design Festival?
Having London Fashion Week here really helped put Somerset House on the map, and vice versa. But the dominating feature was a marquee that the public couldn't get access to. At the Design Festival, what happens in the courtyard will be a public event. And similarly, we'll also help the Festival to take its next step forward.

Will the public have access to Makerversity?
In 2016, there will be 250 artists and makers in residence. A series of rooms on the ground floor of the New Wing will become public project spaces. The pilot example is The Unseen, a materials innovation studio. We'll have an arcade of constantly changing happenings. A cultural souk, if you will.

What role does the Courtauld Gallery play in all this?
It brings a different crowd in. But you'd be surprised by how many people come to see the Goya drawings and also want to catch Secret 7" or Pick Me Up.

What do you hope will be your personal stamp?
Today, if you stopped 10 people in the street and asked, 'What's Somerset House?' you would get 10 disparate answers. I'd like that to change. Somerset House will always mean different things to different people, but I hope that in time the 10 answers feel like 10 parts of a whole. EH

11 Somerset House Strand WC2R 1LA
(See page 99)

For big breakfast
12 Balthazar
4–5 Russell Street WC2B 5HZ
020 3301 1155
balthazarlondon.com

The high-ceilinged outpost of the famous New York brasserie. Try hazelnut waffles for breakfast.

For dinner
13 Barrafina
10 Adelaide Street WC2N 4HZ
020 7440 1456
barrafina.co.uk

The Covent Garden branch of the stellar tapas restaurant.

For drinks then dinner
14 Compagnie des Vins Surnaturels
6 Neal's Yard WC2H 9DP
020 7734 7737
cvssevendials.com

This comfortable restaurant serves plates of cheese and charcuterie, and excellent meat and fish dishes. Bury yourself in the thrilling wine list.

For secret drinks
15 Experimental Cocktail Club
13a Gerrard Street W1D 5PS
020 7434 3559
chinatownecc.com

This romantic bar in bustling Chinatown is hard to get into, but worth it for the low lights, velvet seats, sensational cocktails, and terrifyingly cool staff.

For ice cream
16 Gelatorino
2 Russell Street WC2B 5JD
020 7240 0746
gelatorino.com

Reminiscent of an upmarket Italian gelateria, this offers a regularly changing menu of freshly made, unctuous ice cream. Granitas and ice cream sandwiches also available. Busy in summer.

Left, the marble counter at tapas bar Barrafina

Below, Skye Gyngell's Spring dining room

For quick lunch
17 Kanada-Ya
64 St Giles High Street WC2H 8LE
020 7240 0232
kanada-ya.com

This cute, simply designed Japanese restaurant serves a short menu of delicious tonkotsu ramen, rice balls and sake. Manga cartoons are splashed across the back wall. Service is friendly but expect queues.

For lunch
18 Lima Floral
14 Garrick Street WC2E 9BJ
020 7240 5778
limafloral.com

This is Peruvian mega-chef Virgilio Martinez's second restaurant in London. A fresh-looking white and sea blue space with a giant mural, it serves up wonderful ceviche and meat skewers prepared by head chef Robert Ortiz.

For a sophisticated drink
19 Scarfes Bar at Rosewood London
High Holborn WC1V 7EN
020 3747 8611
scarfesbar.com

A brilliant place for a quick cocktail or madder 'potion of the month', this bar's luscious design is by Martin Brudnizki and includes semi-circular booths, low yellow ochre lighting, and paintings by the bar's inspiration, the renowned caricaturist Gerald Scarfe.

For elegant lunch
20 Spring
Somerset House
Lancaster Place WC2R 1LA
020 3011 0115
springrestaurant.co.uk

Skye Gyngell's seasonal Italian food is elegant but expensive, served in a pretty dining room blanketed in fresh white paint, with white pillars and tablecloths, high ceilings and salmon pink chairs.

For coffee
21 Timberyard
7 Upper St Martin's Lane
WC2H 9DL
timberyardlondon.com

An award-winning café known for its serious approach to tea, coffee and cake, Timberyard also provides a downstairs exhibition space and an embracing attitude towards co-workers with laptops.

BOOK A ROOM

For comfort and convenience
22 The Hoxton Holborn
199–206 High Holborn WC1V 7BD
020 7661 3000
thehoxton.com/london/holborn

For timeless grandeur
23 Rosewood London
252 High Holborn WC1V 7EN
020 7781 8888
rosewoodhotels.com/en/london

The media sounded the death knell for Charing Cross Road after Murder One, London's only dedicated specialist crime bookshop, folded back in 2009. Barely a month earlier, its neighbour Shipley's, the art bookseller, started shipping out. But the decline of 'Charing Corpse Road' really began a decade earlier with the disappearance of the women's bookshop Silver Moon, followed by Waterstones and Borders.

Construction on the city's Crossrail line, which turned the thoroughfare's already chaotic junction with Oxford Street into a dusty tangle of hoarding, should have driven consumers away for good. After all, it brought with it the much derided cleansing of Denmark Street, London's alluringly decrepit Tin Pan Alley. And it was blamed for the recent shuttering of Blackwell's, after all that noisy construction ground footfall nearly to a halt.

But to paraphrase a legendary author whose books are still available at the remaining few dealers, the reports of Charing Cross's death have been greatly exaggerated.

Among the four booksellers that remain between Leicester Square and Tottenham Court Road station, there's a pervading feeling that, per Nietzsche, that which does not kill them makes them stronger.

"People who like books like browsing for books," says Sara MacKillop, manager at Koenig Books, still standing in a David Chipperfield-designed corner property at 80 Charing Cross Road. "They look at those recommendations from Amazon and say, 'I don't like that at all.' Ordering books is very personal. Our customers come in and find things they didn't know they wanted."

MacKillop likens the art and architecture specialist to a reference library. "I know it sounds old fashioned," she says, "but people don't just look for the books they want, they look at the books on either side in the shelves, and that broadens their interests."

†

Charing Corpse Road ?

London's bookshop hotspot might have slimmed down in recent years but the best booksellers on and around Charing Cross Road continue to blaze a trail

While she mourns the passing of peers like Borders, which had an unparalleled magazine section, and Zwemmers, the first shop in the UK to exhibit paintings by Picasso in a gallery above the shop, MacKillop is also optimistic. The comic and culture bookshop Magma, a neighbour in Seven Dials, recently opened in a bigger, more beautiful space in Shorts Gardens. And of course there's Foyles, also bigger and more beautiful after a rebuild by architects Lifschutz Davidson Sandilands.

Any Amount of Books is still on the radar for rare books. The same goes for Quinto, the second-hand bookshop at 72 Charing Cross Road that recently reopened its basement floor with fresh stock. Quinto sells not only hard-to-source titles on music, dance, folklore and shamanism, but also banks of antique books for home décor and set design.

"On the first Tuesday of every month we change all our stock here and we always have a queue outside the door of people waiting to see what they can pick up on that day," Quinto manager Walter Kraut recently told a reporter for *The Bookseller*. "It is quite exciting. I feel like Charing Cross Road has still retained its reputation as a bookselling destination."

"More people selling books is only a good thing," agrees MacKillop. She says a great chunk of Koenig's traffic is attracted to the constantly changing stock, special offers that often undercut even Amazon, and a line in art-exhibition catalogues available nowhere else in town or online.

Meanwhile, at the recently reopened Tottenham Court Road station, the hoards are emerging once again into a landscape happily free of detours and rabbit holes. "The road will never be smart like Lamb's Conduit Street," says MacKillop, "but the Crossrail can only make it nicer." Famous last words? If only to make way for a renaissance. **EH**

CLERKENWELL

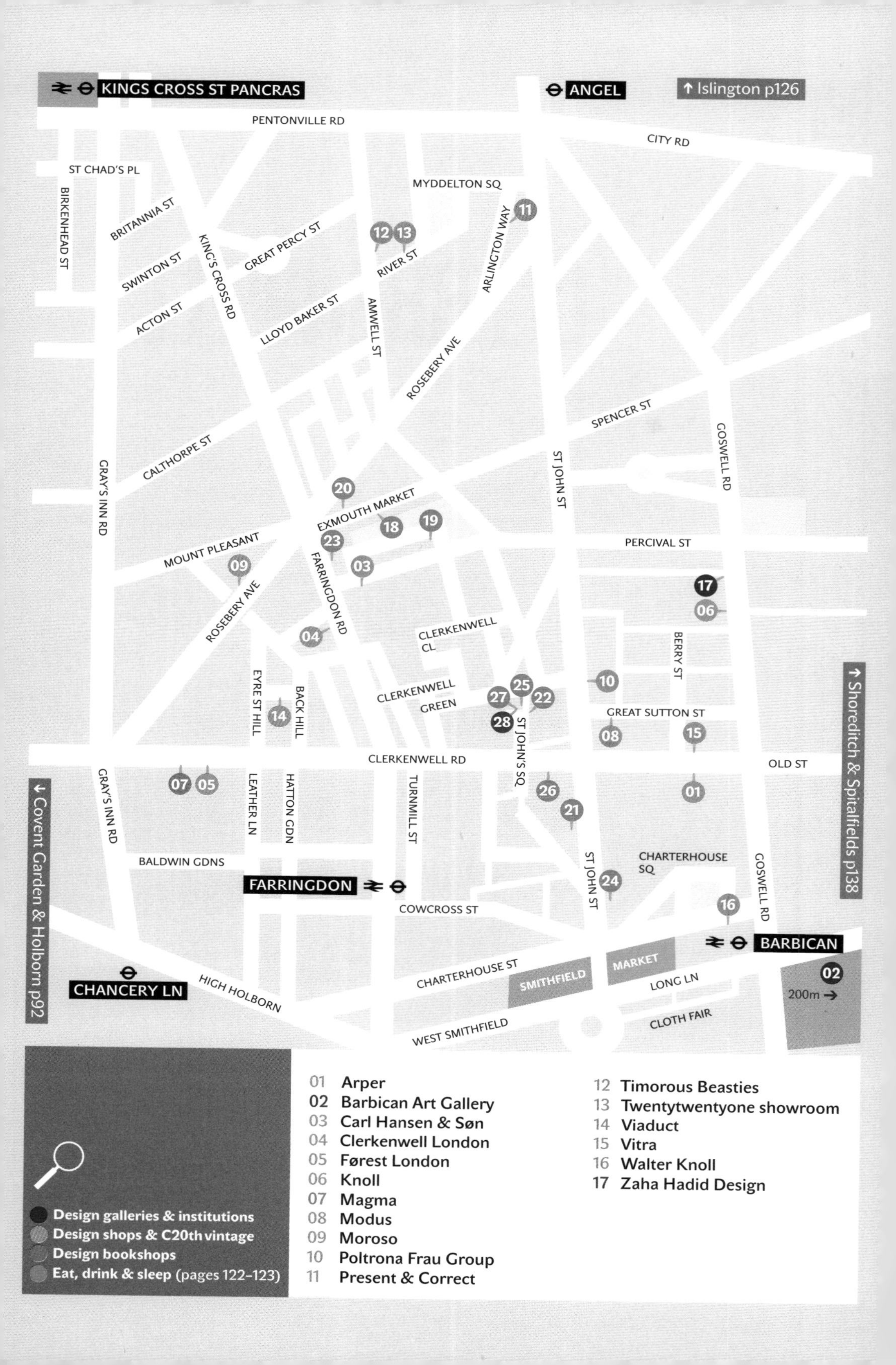
KINGS CROSS ST PANCRAS
ANGEL
↑ Islington p126
PENTONVILLE RD
CITY RD
ST CHAD'S PL
BIRKENHEAD ST
MYDDELTON SQ
BRITANNIA ST
KING'S CROSS RD
GREAT PERCY ST
SWINTON ST
ACTON ST
RIVER ST
ARLINGTON WAY
LLOYD BAKER ST
AMWELL ST
ROSEBERY AVE
CALTHORPE ST
SPENCER ST
GOSWELL RD
ST JOHN ST
GRAY'S INN RD
EXMOUTH MARKET
MOUNT PLEASANT
PERCIVAL ST
FARRINGDON RD
ROSEBERY AVE
CLERKENWELL CL
BERRY ST
CLERKENWELL GREEN
EYRE ST HILL
BACK HILL
GREAT SUTTON ST
ST JOHN'S SQ
CLERKENWELL RD
OLD ST
↑ Shoreditch & Spitalfields p138
← Covent Garden & Holborn p92
GRAY'S INN RD
LEATHER LN
HATTON GDN
TURNMILL ST
ST JOHN ST
CHARTERHOUSE SQ
GOSWELL RD
BALDWIN GDNS
FARRINGDON
COWCROSS ST
BARBICAN
CHANCERY LN
HIGH HOLBORN
CHARTERHOUSE ST
SMITHFIELD
MARKET
LONG LN
200m →
WEST SMITHFIELD
CLOTH FAIR
Design galleries & institutions
Design shops & C20th vintage
Design bookshops
Eat, drink & sleep (pages 122–123)
01 Arper
02 Barbican Art Gallery
03 Carl Hansen & Søn
04 Clerkenwell London
05 Førest London
06 Knoll
07 Magma
08 Modus
09 Moroso
10 Poltrona Frau Group
11 Present & Correct
12 Timorous Beasties
13 Twentytwentyone showroom
14 Viaduct
15 Vitra
16 Walter Knoll
17 Zaha Hadid Design

Clerkenwell

A postwar warehouse surplus made this area outside the City gates an ideal habitat for architects, who settle here in record numbers, and especially for purveyors of heavy furnishings. European manufacturers have gravitated to Clerkenwell as a result, showing their jumbo sofas and contract office configurations in the post-industrial setting Londoners love. New arrival Carl Hansen & Søn coveted a former printing works for years before making it the setting of its first London flagship. To the north, Timorous Beasties, Twentytwentyone and Present & Correct help make Amwell Village a destination of its own.

01 Arper
11 Clerkenwell Road EC1M 5PA
020 7253 0009
arper.com
Mon–Fri 9:30–6

Principally aimed at the trade, members of the public are free to explore this open-plan showroom, designed by 6A Architects in bleached wood, cast aluminium and industrial concrete. It reflects the precision with which Arper designs its furniture lines, such as Lievore Altherr Molina's Duna, Leaf and Catifa chairs, which made the brand famous.

02 Barbican Art Gallery
Barbican Centre, Silk St EC2Y 8DS
020 7638 4141
barbican.org.uk/artgallery
Mon–Sat 10–6, Thu–Fri 10–9

Loved and hated in equal measures, the Barbican is a masterpiece of the Brutalist style, and in recent years its public art facility, the Barbican Centre, has blossomed. The free-of-charge Curve gallery is busy even on Monday mornings, while the Barbican Art Gallery does battle with the V&A and National Portrait Gallery for revered architecture, design, art and photography exhibitions.

03 Carl Hansen & Søn
16 Bowling Green Lane EC1R 0BD
020 7632 7587
carlhansen.com
Mon–Fri 9–5

You've heard the name, sure, but how often have you actually sat in a Hans Wegner chair? Or felt the butter-smooth surface of his extendable dining tables? Manufacturer Carl Hansen has set up its first and only London flagship for this purpose only. Accessed by a spiral staircase in a converted newspaper printer's, the showroom has the entire Wegner oeuvre, plus seating by

Family chair
Knud Erik Hansen,
Carl Hansen & Søn

The furniture manufacturer Carl Hansen & Søn is synonymous with Hans Wegner and his archetypal Danish seating. In the 1940s, the small family business from Odense, Denmark, began collaborating with Wegner and saw him through the design of his CH25 easy chair and the CH24 Wishbone chair, now ubiquitous worldwide. Since Carl's grandson Knud Erik Hansen took the helm in 2002, the company has expanded its holdings, relaunched midcentury classics like Wegner's CH88 chair and commissioned new design. In May 2015, Hansen launched his newest showroom, in a former newspaper printers in Clerkenwell.

Why London and why now?
London is the most important city in Europe and also where we do the most business. It's the environment for architecture and design, so here we have to do something excellent.

And why Clerkenwell?
This place caught my eye immediately. It was in terrible condition but it's a fabulous structure. My wife and I live in a home from 1670, so we have a soft spot for listed buildings. Here we're in a quiet lane, across from the best pub in London, in a beautiful environment.

Would you consider this new flagship to be a gallery or a showroom?
I'd love to call it a gallery. We don't sell out of here – it's purely for show. We're not here to snatch customers away from our dealers. The fun part about the furniture is that it's very classic, alongside a new era of products that are a little more wild, and you can see how they fit into the heritage environment. There's a lot of history and soul. Like us – we're 108 years old.

Are we now seeing Carl Hansen & Søn coming to a turning point?
We're not a staid company. We're a company on the move. Most Danish companies are not very big, and we decided three years ago that we need to be big in order to survive. Our new factory in Denmark is three times the size of our old one, and we keep adding new products. Since acquiring Rud Rasmussen, the

Ole Wanscher and new products by Thomas Bo Kastholm and Tadao Ando. (See left)

04 Clerkenwell London
155 Farringdon Road EC1R 3AD
020 3675 8847
clerkenwell-london.com
Mon-Wed 10-6.30, Thu-Fri 10-8,
Sat-Sun 11-5

Launched in summer 2015, Clerkenwell London is an ambitious retail venture centred around carefully composed displays housing beautifully made homeware items, sourced from around the world and selected with quality, craftsmanship and longevity in mind. Staff can talk you through the stories behind, for example, the hand-blown glassware, faceted ceramics, tactile textiles or the tabletop covered in sumptuous stationery. The ambition comes with the addition of neighbouring rooms of women's wear, own-brand fragrance, bespoke furniture, men's tailoring, a wine room, restaurant and bar, and even a spa. All they need now are some hotel rooms.

05 Førest London
115 Clerkenwell Road EC1R 5BY
020 7242 7370
forestlondon.com
Mon-Fri 11-7, Sat 12-5

Eva Coppens' devotion to Dutch and Scandi furniture greats goes back to her early life in Holland. Now London-based, she is familiar with the commute by van and restores her haul expertly. Her stock is impeccable, original and dainty enough for petite City flats, as well as often blessed with concealed doors and shelves.

06 Knoll
91 Goswell Road EC1V 7EX
020 7236 6655
knoll-int.com
Mon-Fri 9-5.30

There are 75 years of history under this roof, the product of Hans Knoll's business savvy, his wife

Florence's ties to Mies van der Rohe and the enduring designs of modernists like Jens Risom and Eero Saarinen. The showroom posts the odd reminder of its rich heritage and hosts the occasional exhibition or provocative debate to support the exchange of ideas.

07 Magma
117–119 Clerkenwell Road EC1R 5BY
020 7242 9503
magmabooks.com
Mon–Sat 10–7

Alongside its stock of arty books, magazines and miscellany, Magma also does guilty-pleasure typography tomes and pictogram T-shirts, as well as a kids' section that blends in with the adults because the toys appeal to everyone.

08 Modus
28–29 Great Sutton Street EC1V 0DS
020 7490 1358
modusfurniture.co.uk
Mon–Fri 10–6

This home-grown furniture company has launched some of the most memorable designer collaborations in recent years, not least due to its dedication to tapping local talent and a growing number of international names. The tiny Clerkenwell floor has a stripped-back chic courtesy of creative director Michael Sodeau, all the better for displaying the latest merchandise.

09 Moroso
7–15 Rosebery Avenue EC1R 4SP
020 3328 3560
moroso.it
Mon–Fri 9–5

Furniture producer Moroso has a reputation for getting designers to let their eccentricities hang out. In 2010 it opened this expansive Clerkenwell showroom space, dreamed up by Patricia Urquiola, who injected it with an otherworldly wonder that's infectious. Unsurprisingly, Urquiola's designs get pride of place here, colourful and

purveyor of Kaare Klint, we carry an unbroken line of architects since the 1930s, which shows you exactly where we come from and where we're going. We've commissioned contemporary architects like Tadao Ando because we want to work with an architect who's still alive.

Now that you've got flagships across Europe, Asia and America, what's your goal for the company?
To be able to stay independent. If we're not moving internationally, we'll die. And I get claustrophobic if I'm not doing business outside Denmark.

Why does Denmark punch above its weight in terms of design?
We're a very small country and we've always worked and traded internationally. We speak many languages. It's in our blood to get out. Yet people in the furniture industry are very laidback. But the Danish furniture market is big, and many companies have felt that was enough, so a lot of them are closing.

Have you ever wondered what would have happened had you not gone into the family business?
I'd most probably be back in the Far East, where I lived and worked for many years. But I'm very happy that fate has led me here. I went to my brother to sell my shares and he said no, so I bought his shares instead. Somewhere there was a divine plan. EH

03 Carl Hansen & Søn
16 Bowling Green Lane EC1R 0BD (See page 109)

eye-catching as they are. The showroom is geared towards the contract market but the public is welcome to browse.

10 Poltrona Frau Group
St John Street EC1V 4UD
020 7014 5980
poltronafraugroup.com
Mon–Fri 8.30–5.30

Poltrona Frau is at the top of its game, and that's saying something after 100 years in the competitive business of modern Italian furniture. This is one of a dozen temples to Italian interiors in Clerkenwell, but Poltrona Frau doesn't get lost in this elegant Victorian warehouse on St John Street. It has the lure of a boutique, with intimate room sets (Cappellini and Cassina dominate) demonstrating the visual heft of its stock.

11 Present & Correct
23 Arlington Way EC1R 1UY
020 7278 2460
presentandcorrect.com
Tues–Sat 12–6.30

Located in a cosy space in a sweet Georgian terrace in the villagey shopping strip behind Sadler's Wells, this stationer avoids the sparkly twee-ness of chains like Paperchase, opting for a look that nods to the past while agreeing with our contemporary expectations of design. There are desktop supplies in delicious colours, accordion files that win awards at design shows, and well considered stationery like letterpress labels and splendid notebooks to keep in stacks for inspiration.

12 Timorous Beasties
46 Amwell Street EC1R 1XS
020 7833 5010
timorousbeasties.com
Mon–Sat 10– 6

Scottish duo Alistair McAuley and Paul Simmons have cornered the market in natural scenes (on natural fibres) with a decidedly contemporary, even macabre,

Nimble expressionists
Patrik Fredrikson & Ian Stallard

Partners Patrik Fredrikson and Ian Stallard are the duo behind design studio Fredrikson Stallard. They met in 1995 while studying at Central Saint Martins, Fredrikson as a furniture designer and Stallard as a ceramicist. Initially they operated independently, but their working practices and creative sensibilities increasingly converged, prompting them to launch their studio together in 2005.

Down an unsuspecting alley off a quiet street in Clerkenwell, a crushed mass of mirror-polished gold aluminium floats above our heads, shooting reflected light throughout the cavernous length of space. Through doors off this alley are the studio and showroom of Fredrikson Stallard, home base of the designers since they converted it in 2012.

The two tall talents greet us on arrival as we peruse the pieces in their showroom, which is more akin to a gallery. Originally a Georgian brass foundry making carriage wheels, and previously the site of a printer, the place was transformed from a dirty, windowless enclave to a slick, spacious studio. The duo's work sits confidently within this environment – an ensemble of pieces that have been described as "fairy tales for grown-ups", albeit tales that are laced with "underlying themes of opulent and sensual darkness".

The crushed-aluminium concept in the entrance continues along one wall with Hurricane Mirror (2014), the reflected spotlights dancing off every curve. In contrast, on the floor is the perfect linearity of the Diptych Table (2005) in glass, steel and black and white acrylic, sitting alongside a crated object ready to be dispatched to a client. A large item hides beneath dustsheets, confidential to our glaring eyes. Iris (2011) also keeps a watchful eye from the wall, the mesmerising giant circular structure beaming refracted light through a spiralling lens of Swarovski crystals.

The design magic originates from the other side of an elbow-height wall, lined with models and samples.

Fredrikson and Stallard work alongside four others, bathed in natural light from the windows along the back wall. Outside, a rather awkward light well has been transformed into a precious pocket of outdoor space, a sort of urban oasis with a welcome injection of nature from the young silverbirch trees and an exquisite Japanese maple.

We take a seat upstairs in an altogether more comfortable space. Happy in their domain, we discuss their approach to design and their motivations. "We don't want to fill the world with more stuff that is the same. What's the point in producing variations of the same thing?" offer the duo in support of their work within the bespoke and editions side of design. Stallard continues, "We are not modernist in our approach – we're more conceptual, and for us it's all about expressionism. We need more stimulation than 'form follows function'."

Fabricating their creations to exacting standards requires huge trust in their collaborators, with whom they are often exploring what is possible. While the studio is also responsible for projects with brands such as Swarovski, Chanel, Veuve Clicquot, Brioni and Gieves & Hawkes, one senses that this dapper duo is most happy when pursuing a joint fascination with materials in combination with unfamiliar and challenging processes. Fredrikson and Stallard admit to the great sense of freedom enjoyed when alone in creative endeavour. Pushing the envelope with uncompromising autonomy is where their hearts beat.

Since 2006, design gallerist David Gill (see page 75) has represented Fredrikson Stallard and positioned their pieces amid the international collectors market. Despite their design training and the underlying functionality in their work, Gill refers to them as artists. I asked the designers how best to describe them. "There isn't necessarily a word," offers Fredrikson, suggesting they occupy the nimble and somewhat hybrid territory between art and design. Stallard adds, "We create things and come up with ideas for spaces and objects. Aesthetic and contextual issues drive us." Reflecting on possible adjectives, Fredrikson muses, "Eventually, we would like to be the adjective." **MF**

edge. At their only English flagship (the other is in Glasgow), they'll happily point out the weft of a weave, the hand-painted overlay of a digital print or the un-replicated design on a roll of wallpaper.

13 Twentytwentyone showroom
18c River Street EC1R 1XN
020 7837 1900
twentytwentyone.com
Mon-Sat 9.30-5.30

Twentytwentyone has a shopfront on the high-footfall boulevard of Upper Street (see page 131), but at its secluded Amwell Village showroom you get more freedom and more space to test out the big-impact lighting and the range of classic chairs from leading European brands, plus the vast modern sofas and rugs you won't find at the smaller location.

14 Viaduct
1-10 Summers Street EC1R 5BD
020 7278 8456
viaduct.co.uk
Mon-Fri 9.30-6, Sat 10.30-4

In this calm, double-height converted 1930s print house, Viaduct plugs away at assembling a top-notch collection of new furniture and lighting, as well as reissued furnishings by heavyweights of the past century. Viaduct thankfully transcends the trends, selling a well-considered selection of what owner James Mair and his team have sourced internationally. And you can rest assured that you're buying into quality and longevity.

15 Vitra
30 Clerkenwell Road EC1M 5PQ
020 7608 6200
vitra.com
Mon-Thurs 9-5:30, Fri 9-5

You can't buy direct from the showroom for Vitra – the Swiss owned company founded in the mid-20th century to license designs by Charles and Ray Eames and George Nelson for the European market and now pioneer of innovative future classics – but the public are welcome to browse the collections, and staff will inform you of your nearest dealer should you wish to place an order. Keep an eye out for its infamous mid-winter one day sale, when people are known to camp overnight to pick up one of the amazing bargains.

16 Walter Knoll
42 Charterhouse Square
EC1M 6EA
020 7796 5950
walterknoll.de
Mon-Fri 9-6

Like many showrooms in this area, this German brand has a strong foothold in the contract market to which this space is geared. However, despite its rather austere appearance, the public are welcome to visit and view their range for the home. It's worth pointing out that every designer they work with is male and, dare I say it, the choices are distinctly masculine with lots of leather and muted tones, linear forms and, well, a certain formality that may divide opinion.

17 Zaha Hadid Design
101 Goswell Road EC1V 7EZ
020 7253 5147
zaha-hadid-design.com
Tues-Sat 1-6

The gallery space and shop displaying the furniture and design of one of the UK's most prominent architects has been left raw, save for a staircase descending like a series of vertebrae. Upstairs are Hadid's vast sweeps of furniture, so dizzying to wander around, you rue the no-touch policy as you seek somewhere to steady yourself. Downstairs is an array of swooping tabletop designs and jewellery, the function of which you'll have to enlist an assistant to explain.

Open house

The contract showrooms that once dominated Clerkenwell are widening their reach beyond trade-only to a new generation of walk-ins

Six years ago, when Walter Knoll opened a discreet but determined presence in London, there was never any question the manufacturer would lease space near Smithfield Market in Clerkenwell. The area, industry-watchers say, has the highest concentration of architects in the world, let alone the country. For a brand that makes most of its sales through contract work, commissioned by architects to furnish multi-level office complexes and hotels, it was a strategic real estate move.

"For the contract market, Clerkenwell was obviously the best place," says David Searcy, Walter Knoll's showroom manager. "If you have a showroom here, by nature it's got to be a contract showroom."

As it celebrates its 150th year in business, Walter Knoll has found itself in good company. Clerkenwell's role as an architects' hub has encouraged trade-focused showrooms to cluster here for decades. Within 10 blocks of its Charterhouse Square address you'll find Modus, Poltrona Frau, Vitra, Arper, even its erstwhile sister brand Knoll.

The other side of that is that the contract-retail landscape can seem forbidding to the average consumer. Windows aren't dressed with trinkets and gadgetry to attract spontaneous drop-ins. The pièce de résistance might be a three-metre-long office desk. There are no price tags, nor a cash register – money never changes hands on the premises. "The area is not the place to be for residential sales," says Searcy, "because it's not a residential area."

That fact is changing, however slowly. And to keep up with the numbers of young professionals moving into live-work spaces, Barbican towers and refurbished industrial blocks, contract showrooms have begun to quietly court the public. They're more closely following the model of crossover retailers like Vitra, with its engaging space

Previous page, Antibodi loungers by Patricia Urquiola, Moroso showroom, Clerkenwell

Below, Saari seating by Lievore Altherr Molina, Arper showroom, Clerkenwell

Left, wall of chairs, Vitra showroom, Clerkenwell

on Clerkenwell Road and its annual sale, for which residents queue up for hours. When Carl Hansen opened its first London flagship on Bowling Green Lane, CEO Knud Erik Hansen pitched it as a refuge for admirers of Danish greats like Hans Wegner, a place to look, touch and even snuggle into a lounger with a coffee. If a customer then wants to buy, he can do so through a Carl Hansen distributor like Skandium or Twentytwentyone. By contrast, brands like Modus sell only through the Modus store on Great Sutton Street.

Arper and Moroso, which recently won the contract to outfit London's new Google offices, are especially good at the welcome. Staffers at Moroso are separated from the product (designers include Antonio Citterio, Nendo and Patricia Urquiola) by a glass wall, but pop up immediately when the door opens. As sales associate Michela Novara says, "A lot of times architects will send by clients to see the product – it's better to view it in person than in the brochure. But just as often we'll have a private customer, and we're equipped to sell to them straight away."

Even Searcy, at Walter Knoll, will offer coffee and conversation to private customers. Then, if they want to splash out, he'll direct them to distributors like Aram and Coexistence. "We keep the doors open when it's warm enough," says Searcy. "We want to make the process transparent." Eventually he'd like to get Walter Knoll the name recognition among Londoners that it has in Germany and Western Europe. "Our furniture is popular with residential customers throughout Europe – it's just not so well known in the UK... yet." EH

"There are no price tags, nor a cash register – money never changes hands on the premises"

To pig out
18 Blackfoot
46 Exmouth Market EC1R 4QE
020 7837 4384
blackfootrestaurant.co.uk

A must for meatheads, this white tiled and petrol blue former pie and mash shop on Exmouth Market is a piggy paradise. Snack on finocchiona, eat as much as you can from the weekend brunch menu, or share a pile of porchetta and leaves for lunch or dinner.

For breakfast bounty
19 Bourne & Hollingsworth
42 Northampton Road EC1R 0HU
020 3174 1156
bandhbuildings.com

Beautiful airy conservatory space packed with greenery and elegant floral printed armchairs. Food, served all day, is a mixture of comfort and classic, with a breakfast menu including potato hash, bubble and squeak, French toast and eggs Royale.

For snacky lunch
20 Caravan
11–13 Exmouth Market EC1R 4QD
020 7833 8115
caravanexmouth.co.uk

Rammed at weekends around brunchtime, but a quick weekday lunch at the original of the two Caravans will reward you with things like lip-smackingly good cornbread with chipotle butter, ham hock croquettes, and pickled radishes. The interior, wooden and monochrome painted, is simple but pleasing.

For hunky dinner
21 Foxlow
69–73 St John Street EC1M 4AN
020 7014 8070
foxlow.co.uk

Fairly small, simply designed wooden and black leather set-up and a favourite with local City boys for the great hunks of meat coming out of the kitchen. Hawksmoor's sister restaurant.

Left, greenery galore at Bourne & Hollingsworth

Above, the elegant dining room at The Modern Pantry

For one bite lunch
25 Sushi Tetsu
12 Jerusalem Passage EC1V 4JP
020 3217 0090
sushitetsu.co.uk

This dainty restaurant, run by husband and wife Harumi and Toru Takahashi, seats just seven and serves expertly made sushi and famous 'one bite' dishes. It's a big favourite with both chefs and locals.

For coffee and a pastry
26 Workshop Coffee
27 Clerkenwell Road EC1M 5RN
020 7253 5754
workshopcoffee.com

Top notch, wooden, and the original London outpost of this Australian café group. Expect natural wine, craft beer, moreish pastries and a range of award-winning coffees.

For cosy drinks
27 The Zetter Townhouse
49–50 St John's Square EC1V 4JJ
020 7324 4550
thezettertownhouse.com

Consistently fabulous cocktails thought up by Tony Conigliaro, served in seductive country-house-style surroundings – plush cushions, soft leather, flattering lighting, old books. Date-worthy.

For pleasing breakfast
22 The Modern Pantry
47–48 St John's Square EC1V 4JJ
020 7553 9210
themodernpantry.co.uk

Stimulating comfort food in a breezy setting. Try breakfast fruit salad in rose and lime syrup.

For quality dinner
23 Quality Chop House
88–94 Farringdon Road EC1R 3EA
020 7278 1452
thequalitychophouse.com

Hearty cooking with keen and knowledgeable staff. Former working man's 'eating house' with black and white check floor and high wooden pews. Check out the deli.

For vigorous dinner
24 St John
26 St John Street EC1M 4AY
020 7251 0848
stjohnrestaurant.com

The founding member of British nose-to-tail dining, Fergus Henderson serves wood pigeon, kid faggots and dripping toast. The restaurant sports a clean, white, industrial design, much mimicked since.

BOOK A ROOM

For comfortable charm
28 The Zetter Townhouse
49–50 St John's Square EC1V 4JJ
020 7324 4567
thezettertownhouse.com/clerkenwell

ISLINGTON

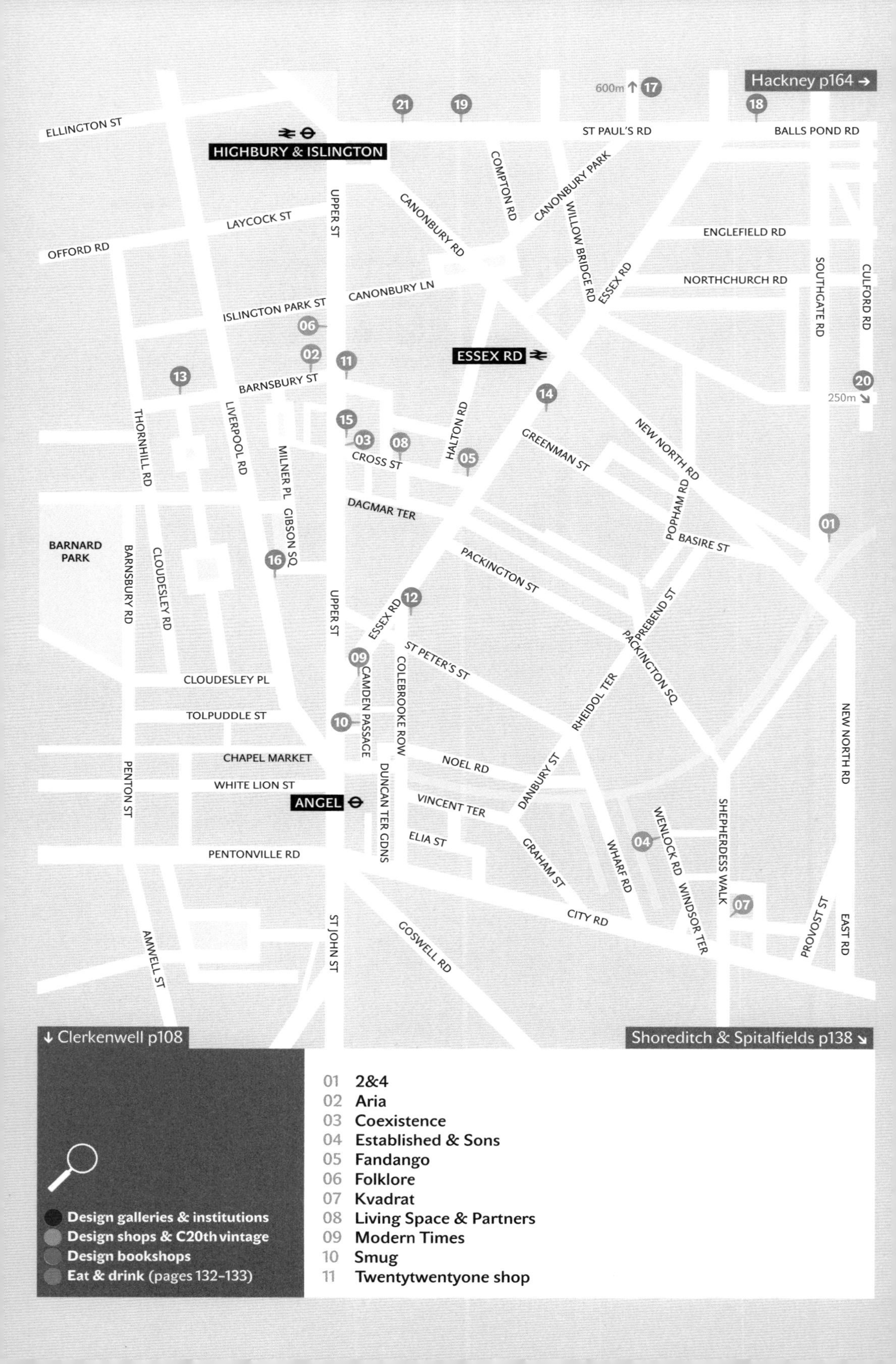

01 **2&4**
02 **Aria**
03 **Coexistence**
04 **Established & Sons**
05 **Fandango**
06 **Folklore**
07 **Kvadrat**
08 **Living Space & Partners**
09 **Modern Times**
10 **Smug**
11 **Twentytwentyone shop**

Islington

Somebody had to furnish the homes of the new, gentrifying class in Islington, which continues on the up after its postwar decline. Luckily it's nothing but quality. The Georgian terraces around Canonbury survive as showcases for Scandi classics and clever, new creations. Close to Islington Green, Camden Passage has a delightful antique market and a strip of plucky independent shops. The canalside warehouses get a more experimental type of tenant in Established & Sons, Kvadrat and 2&4.

01 **2&4**
2-4 Southgate Road N1 3JW
020 7254 5202
2mdesign.co.uk/2m_shop.html
Tues-Fri 9-6.30, Sat 10-6, Sun 11-5

This canal-side former factory is expansive in size and scope, an airy setting for midcentury furniture and retro teaware. Designed by owners Maurice Nugent and Mia Fihnborg, it gives the furnishings within a contemporary context. It might be written off as your average vintage repository if not for the lighting and glasswork thrown into the mix.

02 **Aria**
Barnsbury Hall, Barnsbury Street N1 1PN
020 7704 6222
ariashop.co.uk
Mon-Sat 10-6.30, Sun 12-5

Aria has been serving Islington's bourgeois pioneers for over 25 years, selling contemporary interior products and gifts. The building itself is a joy, with its vaulted gothic ceilings, Georgian brick and light wells, and umpteen nooks and levels to explore. A new building is going up across the road on a plot that has been vacant since 1941, and this will house a new concept gallery space for events, pop-ups and product launches.

03 **Coexistence**
288 Upper Street N1 2TZ
020 7354 8817
coexistence.co.uk
Mon-Sun 11-5

Coexistence has operated for the trade for decades, but recently it opened to a whole new market of Islingtonian homeowners. Though the premises haven't changed radically, they've gotten slightly homelier and the showroom attendants have been versed in the art of the welcome. This is still the place to put in a job lot of Metro dining chairs by Thomas Sandell for Offecct – Coexistence stocks more than 100 seating brands, including lesser-knowns like Birdman from Holland and the Basque manufacturer Stua. It also operates an in-house exhibition space for brand collaborations. (See pages 128–129)

Contract thriller
Mary Wiggin, *Coexistence*

Back in 1982, a nascent contract-furnishing business called Coexistence settled into Islington's Upper Street, setting a high visual bar for its long-neglected surroundings. As young professionals discovered the neighbourhood, gastropubs emerged and real estate skyrocketed, Coexistence remained a beacon of good taste, informing the increasingly smart interiors nearby. Founders Mary Wiggin and Ross Bull have continued to nurture a faithful clientele from their showroom and satellite spaces – all brilliantly converted by Rivington Street Studio. Mary invited us by to test-drive her stock of Zanotta, Tomoko Azumi and Sibast.

I'm struck by the name Coexistence because you've been coexisting with Islington for such a long time.
When we opened 41 years ago in Bath, 'Coexistence' seemed like a good idea because we were doing modern things, coexisting in a Georgian city. I got hold of people like John Makepeace and Ann Sutton. We found ourselves going back and forth to London for contract clients, so after four years we found a space on Floral Street and eventually bought this showroom on Upper Street for our contract work. Now we've opened it to retail seven days a week. Upper Street has changed a lot. It's become estate-agent-and-hairdresser heaven.

How have you managed to stay yourselves in the changing retail landscape?
We've got a good team of real furniture lovers who really know about tables and chairs. They offer a more sincere proposal to the clients, and I hope that's where we score over our competitors. It's difficult to sell good design with the internet. Architonic is great, but you don't know what you'll find there, and often it's a copy. IKEA have done an Artek stool. That's the sort of thing we're up against.

Could you have enjoyed this longevity anywhere else but Islington?
We're very lucky because we own the premises. If we didn't, we'd be struggling.

Which British designers in particular have you really championed over the years?
When we were in Floral Street we had an exhibition of Matthew Hilton and Jasper Morrison, and I've followed them ever since. Jasper just keeps getting better. He excelled himself recently with a fantastic chair for Emeco that sadly can't be sold in the UK because it's made out of recycled wood, which doesn't meet our fire regulations.

Do you still devote yourself largely to contract work?
Yes, we deal a lot with corporate clients. We've maintained relationships with the BBC, BP, Heathrow, KPMG... We've done so much work for Maggie's Centres – we're furnishing the Nottingham centre now.

You've always had a base of 20th-century classics. Has your offering become more contemporary?
It's a bit of both. We go to all the furniture fairs in order that our sales team knows what's new. It's depressing how many people copy – not knock off, but it's all so derivative. So when we do find something that's innovative, it inspires us all.

What counts as innovative today?
At the Milan Furniture Fair there was an amazing display of rugs from Afghanistan. For all the trouble that's going on there, to then come across these beautiful rugs is something we want to try and promote. Christopher Farr is producing two of them, so we'll try to do something with him. And Nendo have done a beautiful chair for Alias called Twig. **EH**

03 **Coexistence** 288 Upper Street N1 2TZ
(See page 127)

04 Established & Sons
5–7 Wenlock Road N1 7SL
020 7608 0990
establishedandsons.com
Mon–Fri 9.30–5.30

Established & Sons launched in 2005 to elevate contemporary British furniture design, and its portfolio has since grown to include like-minded Europeans such as the Bouroullec brothers and Jaime Hayon. Seeing all the designs in one place is to experience awe. Find the window stencilled with the company logo, then scan along to the right, where you'll eventually find a barely-marked door, across from the Wenlock Arms. Buzz and someone will welcome you into the showroom and give you a knowledgeable tour to boot.

05 Fandango
2 Cross Street N1 2BL
07979 650 805
fandangointeriors.co.uk
Wed–Sat 11–6

Owners Henrietta Palmer and Jonathan Ellis stock an impressive cache of midcentury desks, sunburst mirrors and chrome, as well as eccentric ceramics picked up on scouts to Germany, Benelux and beyond. And an unparalleled collection of 1920s glass and midcentury industrial lighting casts a golden glow, creating a magical antidote to the white-on-white Scandi trend.

06 Folklore
193 Upper Street N1 1RQ
020 7354 9333
shopfolklore.com
Mon–Sat 11–6, Sun 12–5.30

Folklore stocks a collection of inventive, highly tactile objects in wood and paper, as well as fabrics and knits so natural you can almost smell the rawness. Products may be made from chemical-free materials, crafted from reclaimed wood, or infinitely recyclable but the eco agenda evident in Folklore's buying criteria refrains from overtly socking the message to you.

Above, Upper Street store Folklore's throwback chic

Right, glass box views from Twentytwentyone

07 Kvadrat
10 Shepherdess Walk N1 7LB
020 7324 5555
kvadrat.dk
Mon–Thurs 9–5.30, Fri 9–5

In 2009 Danish textile manufacturer Kvadrat opened its boundary-pushing London flagship, designed by David Adjaye with help from graphic designer Peter Saville, and it's worth a visit whatever your personal style. A colosseum-style staircase leads down past a wall of glass in a spectrum of colours to a lower-level space where a seemingly bare back wall is actually fitted with pull-out cabinets that house all of their fabric collections.

08 Living Space & Partners
36 Cross Street N1 2BG
020 7359 3950
livingspaceuk.com
Mon–Sat 9.30–6, Sun 12–5

As at every branch of Living Space, each item can be customised to your specifications. Block storage can be wall-mounted, low-slung, configured as a room divider, arranged in stylised designs or transformed into coordinating kitchen cabinetry. Your bed can be appended with any number of shelves, niches or drawers. Or you can have your wardrobe panelled to match your sofa.

09 Modern Times
34A Islington Green N1 8DU
07710 770 214
moderntimesvintage.co.uk
Mon, Thu & Fri 12–6, Wed 9–5,
Sat 10–6, Sun 12–5

Modern Times is housed within a tiny corner location at one end of Camden Passage and is always full of an array of 20th century homewares, principally drinking glasses, tea sets, dinner sets and the occasional item of furniture. Pieces are usually in very good condition and seldom eye-watering in price, making it an ideal place for gifts or the odd indulgence. The owner is very knowledgeable and can source particular items for you, as well as attach a story to your purchase.

10 Smug
13 Camden Passage N1 8EA
020 7354 0253
ifeelsmug.com
Tues 12–5, Wed, Fri 11–6, Thurs 12–7,
Sat 10–6, Sun 12–5

Working designer Lizzie Evans' highly covetable collection of graphic homewares, textiles and stationery give Smug a firm footing in the independent retail scene. Vintage furniture items are also for sale and, with space here being such a premium, cleverly double as displays for the smaller pieces. Evans also goes that extra mile and commissions exclusives from some of Britain's most compelling new designer-makers. Also enjoy a coffee or snack in the tiny basement café.

11 Twentytwentyone shop
274 Upper Street N1 2UA
020 7288 1996
twentytwentyone.com
Mon–Sat 10–6, Sun 11–5

Twentytwentyone's glass-box construction seems to draw in natural light no matter what the weather. A haven for enduring 20th-century design that keeps on top of the latest product developments, this place has always delivered. And what it delivers is dreams. Any chair you've ever coveted will likely be in stock, and all those life-changing storage solutions are here, adorned with goodies for the luckiest of children.

For clever cocktails
12 69 Colebrooke Row
69 Colebrooke Row N1 8AA
07540 528 593
69Colebrookerow.com

Tiny corner premises owned by London cocktail maestro Tony Conigliaro. Booking is vital.

For pub supper
13 Drapers Arms
44 Barnsbury Street N1 1ER
020 7619 0348
thedrapersarms.com

Super pub in a former townhouse whose faithful north London admirers come for its reliably good food – think beef pies and fish of the day – and relaxed atmosphere. The gorgeous bright green bar set against a comfortable wooden interior is its most prominent feature.

For experimental drinks
14 London Cocktail Club
108 Essex Road N1 8LX
020 7580 1960
londoncocktailclub.co.uk

The London Cocktail Club's newest hangout is a dark, cavernous space with lots of nooks for dating couples, and an apothecary tasting room where you will be given a bespoke prescription to sort you out. Look out for the Apothecary Off License shop front.

For an alternative breakfast
15 Ottolenghi
287 Upper Street N1 2TZ
020 7288 1454
ottolenghi.co.uk

Yotam Ottolenghi's original haunt is just the place to kick you into the day ahead. Bright, white, with stacks of breakfast options from za'atar frittata to yoghurt or toast with homemade jams, some of the best granola in London, and a pile of galumphing meringues to take away for afternoon tea.

Neighbourhood haunt Trullo has a very loyal following

For a hearty dinner

16 The Pig & Butcher
80 Liverpool Road N1 0QD
020 7226 8304
thepigandbutcher.co.uk

Just the kind of gastropub you want at the end of your street, this serves a selection of good craft beers, and hearty, mood boosting food like beef dripping on toast, chicken rillettes, Angus beef hash, and rice pudding brulee. Sister to barbecue pub Smokehouse.

For a light lunch

17 Primeur
Barnes Motors,
116 Petherton Road N5 2RT
020 7226 5271
primeurn5.co.uk

Newish neighbourhood joint in Canonbury, fitted out with pared back wooden décor, old velvet theatre chairs and gigantic garage doors that slide back to let in swathes of sunlight. Come for wine and lovely things from the daily changing menu. Open for lunch three days a week only but most nights for dinner.

For a quick dinner

18 Salvation In Noodles
122 Balls Pond Road N1 4AE
020 7254 4534
salvationinnoodles.co.uk

Cutely designed noodle bar, with big, busting bowls of Vietnamese pho, bulging and flavoursome summer rolls, intriguing puddings, locally brewed beers and potent Vietnamese coffee. Fun.

For coffee lovers

19 Sawyer & Gray
290 St Paul's Road N1 2LH
sawyerandgray.co.uk

Perky café with a vintage feel thanks to the eclectic selection of upcycled furniture. Good range of coffee from local roasters Climpson & Sons, and a comforting breakfast and brunch menu with lots of things on toast or with eggs.

For al fresco lunch

20 Towpath Cafe
36 De Beauvoir Crescent N1 5SB
020 7254 7606

The best way to approach this cute, popular little bar and cafe is to saunter along the canal before making a replenishment stop for anything from juice to natural wine, salads and sandwiches, soft-serve ice cream and cake. Hurry along, mind – it's always busy.

For delectable dinner

21 Trullo
300–302 St Paul's Road N1 2LH
020 7226 2733
trullorestaurant.co.uk

Two-floored neighbourhood restaurant that has a stampede of loyal followers. Fresh monochrome design, careful service and a rustic, Italian-inspired menu that always delivers. The best seats are at ground level.

Annual Design

March

Designs of the Year
Design Museum (March–August)
designsoftheyear.com

Each year the Design Museum embarks on the epic task of condensing the year's design feats into one gallery. Encompassing broad themes including transport, digital and architecture, the show divulges the favourites of both the esteemed judges and the public.

RCA Secret
Royal College of Art
secret.rca.ac.uk

This first-come-first-served sale blurs the established with the fledgling, as anonymously designed postcards submitted by world-class artists, designers and architects, and graduating students alike are up for grabs, with the creators revealed after the sale.

April

D&AD Awards Judging Week
The Old Truman Brewery
dandad.org/judging-week-2015

A free, public exhibition of award winning 'commercial creativity' held in east London, alongside events, tours and the D&AD president's lecture series. Exhibited projects span advertising, sound design and beyond, all competing for a coveted D&AD pencil.

Pick Me Up
Somerset House
pickmeuplondon.com

Hosted by Somerset House, annual graphic art fair Pick Me Up is the place to buy editions, discover new galleries and collectives, attend events and hands-on workshops, or simply be inspired by fresh graphic offerings.

May

Collect
Saatchi Gallery
craftscouncil.org.uk/collect

Collect transforms the Saatchi Gallery into a sleek who's who of the contemporary craft scene every May. A great opportunity to buy, discover what's new and meet the makers, from ceramicists to jewellers.

London Craft Week
citywide
londoncraftweek.com

Launched in 2015, London Craft Week puts craft in the spotlight providing insight into the craftsmanship and making processes behind beautiful objects through demonstrations, talks and hands-on sessions.

Clerkenwell Design Week
across Clerkenwell
clerkenwelldesignweek.com

Design-packed May rounds off with Clerkenwell Design Week, a three-day festival with various hub venues around Clerkenwell, complemented by events at local showrooms as well as ambitious installations.

June

London Festival of Architecture
citywide
londonfestivalofarchitecture.org

A month-long festival featuring public projects all over the city, each responding to a theme, with previous editions including 'Work in Progress' and 'Capital'. The resulting projects highlight contemporary issues within architecture.

June & July

SohoCreate
across Soho
sohocreate.co.uk

SohoCreate is a festival encouraging conversation on creativity. The event consists of chats, drinks, performances and discussions all with top UK creatives from broad disciplines including game design, bespoke tailoring and chocolate making, to name a few.

University and college graduate shows
Check individual websites

June and July are packed with graduate showcases. London colleges are joined by other institutions throughout the country who pop-up in the capital to proudly display their designs, providing a chance for everyone to find refreshing new talent.

New Designers
Business Design Centre
www.newdesigners.com

Running for over 30 years, New Designers is a vast graduate showcase at the Business Design Centre in Islington. Split into two parts, the show encompasses jewellery, ceramics, furniture, product and beyond, with awards, events and workshops running in parallel.

Free Range
The Old Truman Brewery
free-range.org.uk

Another opportunity to discover graduate talent from art and design disciplines, this time in east London at the Old Truman Brewery. The show is a career developing opportunity for graduates, and an opportunity for professionals to spot trends and find future stars.

Serpentine Pavilion
Kensington Gardens
serpentinegalleries.org/explore/pavilion

Serpentine Galleries' annual pavilion commission is one of the top-ten most visited architecture and design exhibitions in the world. Each summer the project provides the opportunity for an architectural practice to create an experimental, temporary, outdoor structure.

July & August

Jerwood Makers Open
Jerwood Space
jerwoodvisualarts.org/Jerwood-Makers-Open

The Jerwood Makers Open exhibition showcases the outcomes of a Jerwood Visual Arts initiative which enables emerging applied artists to create personally-led creative commissions with a focus on making, materials and challenging definitions.

September

London Design Festival
citywide
londondesignfestival.com

The annual celebration of all things design, London Design Festival has grown year on year since its inception in 2003, with impressive landmark projects, a hub at the V&A, ever-developing design districts, fairs and partner events sprawling across the city.

Open House London
citywide
openhouselondon.org.uk

For architecture and interior design addicts, Open House London is a unique chance to nose around some of London's finest private buildings for one weekend every September. The festival connects neighbourhoods and develops architectural awareness through direct experience.

October

PAD
Berkeley Square
pad-fairs.com/london

Head to Mayfair for PAD (the Pavilion of Art & Design), a fair for 20th century art, design and decorative arts which runs as part of London's autumn creative season. The objects and artworks within attract collectors, consultants, interior designers and the public.

December

East London Design Show
eastlondondesignshow.co.uk

A design show for trade buyers and Christmas shoppers alike, the East London Design Show has been running for over 20 years as a selling platform for independent product, interior and jewellery designer-makers.

Throughout the year

Midcentury Modern shows
modernshows.com

Midcentury Modern's regular one-day shows selling coveted 20th century furniture and home accessories take place in fittingly appropriate settings including Dulwich College in south London and Erno Goldfinger's Haggerston School in east London.

Events Calendar

SHOREDITCH & SPITALFIELDS

Islington p126
HOXTON
Hackney p164
CREMER ST
EAST RD
PITFIELD ST
HOXTON ST
KINGSLAND RD
RAVENSCROFT ST
HACKNEY RD
COLUMBIA RD
CITY RD
DRYSDALE ST
HOXTON SQ
CORONET ST
Clerkenwell p108
OLD ST
OLD ST
ARNOLD CIRCUS
SHOREDITCH HIGH ST
CALVERT AV
COWPER ST
RIVINGTON ST
CHARLOTTE RD
CURTAIN RD
BOUNDARY ST
BATEMAN'S ROW
TABERNACLE ST
NEW INN YD
REDCHURCH ST
GREAT EASTERN ST
CITY RD
LEONARD ST
BETHNAL GREEN RD
BUNHILL FIELDS
PAUL ST
LUKE ST
HOLYWELL LN
SCLATER ST
CHESHIRE ST
EPWORTH ST
SCRUTTON ST
SHOREDITCH HIGH ST
CLIFTON ST
WORSHIP ST
ALLEN GARDENS
QUAKER ST
FINSBURY SQ
SNOWDEN ST
TRUMAN BREWERY
WILSON ST
APPOLD ST
FOLGATE ST
DRAY WALK
BRICK LN
PRIMROSE ST
HANBURY ST
MOORGATE
BISHOPSGATE
SPITALFIELDS
BRUSHFIELD ST
FOURNIER ST
GUN ST
COMMERCIAL ST
FASHION ST
LIVERPOOL ST
ARTILLERY PASSAGE
LIVERPOOL ST
MOORGATE
WENTWORTH ST
LONDON WALL
ALDGATE EAST
THREADNEEDLE ST
100m
WHITECHAPEL HIGH ST
ALDGATE
Design galleries & institutions
Design shops & C20th vintage
Design bookshops
Eat, drink & sleep (pages 156–157)
01 Ally Capellino
02 Artwords Bookshop
03 Atomic Antiques
04 B Southgate
05 Charlene Mullen
06 Elementary
07 Gallery FUMI
08 Geffrye Museum
09 Goodhood Store
10 House of Hackney
11 Jasper Morrison Shop
12 KK Outlet
13 Klaus Haapaniemi
14 Labour and Wait
15 Lee Broom
16 Ligne Roset City
17 Luna & Curious
18 Material
19 Monologue
20 Nelly Duff
21 One Good Deed Today
22 Pitfield London
23 Ryantown
24 SCP East
25 Squint
26 Tokyobike
27 Tord Boontje Shop
28 Tracey Neuls
29 Two Columbia Road
30 Unto This Last
31 YCN

Shoreditch & Spitalfields

Once upon a time you could make furniture in Shoreditch but you couldn't buy it – not until Sheridan Coakley of SCP started selling his friends' skilled wood pieces from a Curtain Road warehouse. It took decades, but a new generation of crafters, graphic artists and antique dealers have made Shoreditch, and its neighbour Spitalfields, world-famous as a trove for original ideas with handmade post-hipster allure. Day or night, the area bordered by Columbia Road, Redchurch Street and Charlotte Road is prime walking territory and people-watching gold.

01 **Ally Capellino**
9 Calvert Avenue E2 7JP
020 7033 7843
allycapellino.co.uk
Mon–Sat 11–6, Sun 11–5

See page 35 for Notting Hill shop, page 56 for Marylebone shop and pages 58–63 for interview.

02 **Artwords Bookshop**
69 Rivington Street EC2A 3AY
020 7729 2000
artwords.co.uk
Mon–Fri 10.30–7, Sat 11–7, Sun 10–6

See page 167 for Hackney shop.

03 **Atomic Antiques**
125 Shoreditch High Street E1 6JE
020 7739 5923
atomica.me.uk
Tues–Fri 11.30–5.30

This antique dealer has an exceptionally well-considered stock. Of the rich cache of Danish oak armchairs and love seats, the ones with damaged upholstery have been refitted with Paul Smith striped tailoring, repurposed burlap or even lumberjack wool check. The selection of lighting has been tightly curated to include a small selection of Hala desk lamps from Holland and Italian pendants.

04 **B Southgate**
4 The Courtyard, Ezra Street E2 7RH
07905 960792
bsouthgate.co.uk
Sun 9–3

You know you're getting close to Columbia Road's Sunday flower market when you see shoppers strolling away lugging bagfuls of greenery. What you may not notice are the vans hauling chrome display units and aged leather club chairs off site at Ben Southgate's courtyard showroom. Southgate's early-20th-century stock is indisputably true to the look, with an integrity that's not inevitable in London.

NIKE
NIKE

Design Olympians

Edward Barber & Jay Osgerby

Blink and you'd miss it but in the heart of Shoreditch is the understated doorway to the design studio of Barber Osgerby. Founded by Edward Barber and Jay Osgerby in 1996, it has enjoyed considerable success over the years, becoming one of the UK's most prominent design studios. The duo also set up successful architecture and interiors practice Universal Design Studio in 2001, and strategy-based industrial design consultancy MAP in 2012. We sat down with them to discuss some of their defining moments over the past two decades.

We take a seat in their Shoreditch studio in one of a number of rooms spread across various levels. The relaxed double act of Barber and Osgerby change focus from an engrossing design session and cast their minds back to 1996. At that time, the two young upstarts were fresh from their studies in architecture at the Royal College of Art and working out of a flat in the brutalist Trellick Tower in west London.

Much of their early work involved the folding and shaping of sheet material and gave rise to their first piece, the Loop table, produced by Isokon Plus in 1997. Before they knew it, Giulio Cappellini of Cappellini, one of Italy's most avant-garde manufacturers at the time, had spotted and taken on this design. This propelled them into the industry limelight and subsequently spawned commissions from a wealth of international clients. As Barber states, "We may as well have been based in Milan at that time as most of our clients were there." Furthermore, the table was acquired for the collections of the V&A in London and the Metropolitan Museum in New York, and it gave the designers rapid affirmation that they were on the right path.

They cite other key moments, such as 2004 when they won the Jerwood Applied Arts Prize that led to commissions for new furniture for the De La Warr Pavilion on England's south coast. They were becoming known for strong graphic clarity in their designs, which was perfectly captured in the Tab light for Flos in 2008. "This was really our first mass-appeal product," says

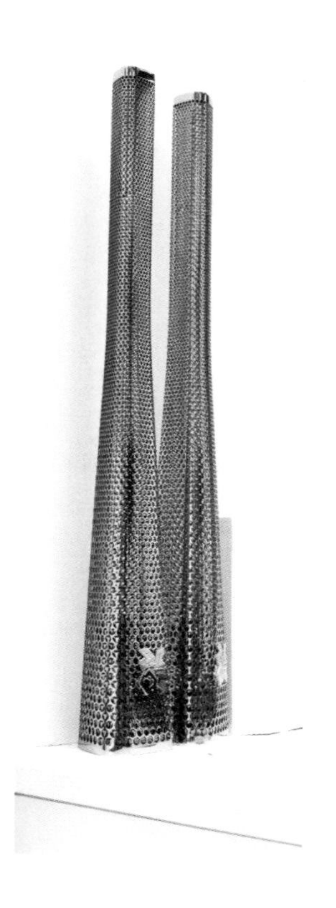

Osgerby. Around the same time, they were heavily engrossed in extensive research for the Tip Ton chair, an injection-moulded plastic chair that addressed posture and improved concentration for school kids. When it launched in 2010, the well priced, cleverly engineered chair gained immediate traction with a broad customer base. "John Lewis sells about 10,000 units per year," exclaims Barber, clearly proud of this volume.

But it was 2012 that propelled the studio into the public realm when their torch for the London Olympics 2012 was paraded for the world to admire. "We never considered how visible the torch would be," says Barber.

These moments make up only a snippet of their output, and they are fortunate to be offered a steady stream of enticing projects. "There is more clarity now in what we do and what we don't do," says Barber.

So why are they based in Shoreditch? They say they recognise it is a convenient location for their team and a significant creative hub in London to attract this talent. That said, most of their clients are located in other countries, which means they regularly need to travel. "But London is our city – the place we started and now home to our young families," states Osgerby. "There is plenty to see and do; great museums, parks and schools; multicultural influences; and all of that on our doorstep."

Barber and Osgerby acknowledge the city's growing expense and, should it become stifling in the future, claim they would just up-and-move to another city or country. But as things stand, London continues to give them everything they need and provides the platform on which many more key moments will be defined. **MF**

At Elementary, a certain purity transcends

05 Charlene Mullen
7 Calvert Avenue E2 7JP
020 7739 6987
charlenemullen.com
Tues-Sat 11-6, Sun 11-5

Charlene Mullen's studio and retail space is on Calvert Avenue, a calm enclave of independent retailers. You may feel you're interrupting the studio workflow on a visit to the shop, but you're very welcome to browse her now-signature cushion range, be it the Scenic collection depicting city skylines and key landmarks, or the enticing blankets and ceramics. Fans of black and white will be drawn to her confident drawn line, which varies from the geometric to the abstract.

06 Elementary
77 Redchurch Street E2 7DJ
020 3487 0980
elementarystore.co.uk
Tues-Sat 11-6, Sun 11-5

Founded in 2014 by Athena Peletidou and Kotaro Kanai, Elementary stocks a beautifully curated selection of interior items, from delicate glass stemware and all-white porcelain teapots and crockery to all-glass lighting and sharp-edged stainless steel side tables – a certain purity transcending it all. One senses that this duo are not pressured by the latest trends, instead following their intuition when sourcing items and favouring the calm over the garish. They also create their own handcrafted furniture and objects, made by local artisans at Peletidou's family-run workshop in north Greece, most of which is displayed in the basement showroom. Elementary is one of those shops that you wish there were more of in our cities, where all too often homogenous brand stores dominate.

07 Gallery FUMI
16 Hoxton Square N1 6NT
020 7490 2366
galleryfumi.com
By appointment only

Despite design gallery FUMI's killer fourth floor view overlooking Hoxton Square, you might feel as if you've fallen down the rabbit hole here, in among urns of Jesmonite that look like marble, rubber vases that appear liquid, and Dentalium shells that feel vaguely threatening. But it's worth making that appointment to see the staggering portfolio by the likes of Max Lamb, Faye Toogood and Sam Orlando Miller.

08 Geffrye Museum
136 Kingsland Road E2 8EA
020 7739 9893
geffrye-museum.org.uk
Tues-Sat 10-5, Sun 12-5

The Geffrye Museum – housed in a block of 18th-century almshouses with a generous swathe of manicured green out front and mazes of period gardens out back – features a collection of quintessentially English rooms arranged in a timeline from 1600 to the present. At its centre is a library and reading room, while a newer wing incorporates a rotunda with an exhibition of 20th-century furnishings, plus a gift shop, event space and basement gallery. The restaurant occupies a contemporary conservatory and benefits from the award-winning walled herb garden it overlooks.

09 Goodhood Store
151 Curtain Road EC2A 3QE
020 7729 3600
goodhoodstore.com
Mon–Fri 10.30–6.30, Sat 10.30–7, Sun 12–6

It's hard to remember a time when Shoreditch shopping consisted of the wonderful SCP and a lonely American Apparel. Now you could browse the day away, and that's precisely what this storefront for online retailer Goodhood is for. Bypass the main-floor apparel and hit the basement, curated with Euro-designed goodies. The tight edit includes top-drawer Hay stationery, &Tradition ceramic pendants, Ferm Living linens and marble-chunk homewares from Menu on Petites Productions tables by Marie Thurnauer. Emerge hours later squinting at the light, your browse having evolved into something much more costly.

10 House of Hackney
131–132 Shoreditch High Street
E1 6JE
020 7739 3901
houseofhackney.com
Mon–Sat 10–7, Sun 11–5

We dare you to make it out of here without a new appreciation for jungle prints. Like the most convincing tropical boutiques, from which we haul all manner of festive souvenirs without a thought for practicality, House of Hackney immerses you in its world and gets you in the mood. Yes, you need that Palmeral bamboo wallpaper and pineapple lamp, and a trip down the spiral staircase to nestle into a coordinating deck chair. It's all beyond whimsical, right out to the street-front florist.

11 Jasper Morrison Shop
24B Kingsland Road E2 8DA
jaspermorrison.com
Mon–Fri 11–5

Don't be intimidated by the buzz-only entrance – you are most welcome here. This snug cube of a shop in the courtyard of eminent designer Jasper Morrison's London studio is like a living encyclopaedia of his product portfolio. Morrison's Cordless DP 01 telephones for Punkt are a clear draw, but he also highlights designs from other 'function over form' designers and manufacturers, like Alessi's citrus juicer, a range of colourful Pentel pens, and the iconic Giannina espresso maker.

12 KK Outlet
42 Hoxton Square N1 6PB
020 7033 7680
kkoutlet.com
Mon–Fri 9–6, Sat 12–5

If you were a hot creative agency with an empty storefront on Hoxton Square, what would you do with it? Amsterdam-based KesselsKramer has spun it into a gallery-bookshop with a monthly rotation of graphic design, illustration and art. There is always thematic merchandise to purchase, and a decent library of art and design tomes, often with a tongue-in-cheek slant.

13 Klaus Haapaniemi
81 Redchurch Street E2 7DJ
020 7739 6777
klaush.com
Tues–Fri 11–7, Sat 11–6, Sun 12–5

Finns have a child's fascination with folk art and fairytales, projecting their fantasies onto the animal kingdom. Klaus Haapaniemi, the millennial's Marimekko, articulates this better than most. Based in London, he and partner Mia Wallenius have been designing fanciful fabrics for upholstery, homewares and rugs since 2010, launching a standalone store on Shoreditch's most newsworthy street a few years later. The bijou boutique is suitably dark and dramatic, an ideal escape from the fashion show on the pavement.

14 Labour and Wait
85 Redchurch Street E2 7DJ
020 7729 6253
labourandwait.co.uk
Tues–Sun 11–6

More than a dozen years ago, Labour and Wait popped up on nearby Cheshire Street selling waxed aprons and feather dusters, enduring products that flew in the face of New Millennium consumerism. The General Store model endured, and Labour and Wait moved to Redchurch Street just as the fashion for sturdy, reliable dry goods was reaching the mainstream. In the process it has played a part in keeping some long-established European manufacturers in the business of, say, enamelware, aluminium dustpans and Kreide dustless blackboard chalk.

15 Lee Broom
95 Rivington Street EC2A 3AY
020 7820 0742
leebroom.com
Mon–Fri 10–6, Sat 11–6, Sun 12–6

What began as the designer's studio eventually expanded into a trade showroom and now retail premises for all to visit. In less than ten years, Lee Broom has built up a sizeable collection of striking and sculptural furniture, lighting and accessories which are artfully displayed across two small floors. (See page 148–149)

16 Ligne Roset City
37–39 Commercial Road E1 1LF
020 7426 9670
ligne-roset-city.co.uk
Mon–Sat 10–6, Sun 12–5

It's wholesale heaven out here on the boundary between creative London and the old garment district – an awkward locale for the typical (well-heeled, West London) Ligne Roset customer, but perfect for backing in a moving van. And there's plenty at this largest London location that you'll want to truck over to yours. The stalwart French manufacturer may still stock some of the same styles that secured it a place in the furniture canon years ago, but a brilliant and always modern range of vibrant suede, velvet and wool upholsteries – plus a growing roster of accessories – keeps it relevant.

17 Luna & Curious
24–26 Calvert Avenue E2 7JP
020 3222 0034
lunaandcurious.com
Mon–Sat 11–6, Sun 11–5

Owners Kaoru Parry, Polly George and Rheanna Lingham have cultivated a space that is as much gallery as shop, tending toward surreal, Wonderland-style displays that leap from the white walls. Fashion junkies will claim this place for their own; the inventive jewellery and irreverent colour-block tights are style coups. But Luna's strong suit is its singular collection of porcelain. Polly George's all-white tabletop ceramics with butterfly appliqués are feats of the kiln. Table settings by We Love Kaoru are equally loveable: classic shapes trimmed in gold with subversive patterns, like the geometric Basilica series, inspired by 17th century Venetian church tiles.

18 Material
1–3 Rivington Street EC2A 3DT
020 7739 1900
materialmaterial.com
Mon–Fri 11–7, Sat 11–6

With Charing Cross increasingly unreliable for books of an artistic bent, someone had to pick up the slack. Enter Joseph Gimlik and Lucy Payne, who launched this 'concept bookshop' as a middle ground between the dusty antiquarians and the grandiose £250-a-tome book boutiques. They support designers and artists of all styles, from twee and painterly to Saul Bass-bold at prices that are affordable even to Shoreditch interns. Material is determined to keep you stocking your shelves

with actual reading material, but there's also a good selection of limited edition prints, as well as tchotchkes, gifts and stationery – the bread and butter of the modern bookstore.

19 Monologue
93 Redchurch Street E2 7DJ
07590 565884
monologuelondon.com
Tues–Sat 10.30–7, Sun 11–6

Monologue calls itself a 'contemporary concept store', selling graphic, colourful and sculptural furniture, lighting, accessories and stationery from a mix of emerging as well as more established designers, some of which are exclusive. La Chance, for example, is a burgeoning French brand known for producing avant-garde furniture for those hunting for a statement.

20 Nelly Duff
156 Columbia Road E2 7RG
020 7033 9683
nellyduff.com
Mon–Fri 9–6, Sat 11–6, Sun 9–4

The artists whose original and limited-edition art gets an airing here come from all over the world, but the overarching theme is the street style and the tattoo'd aesthetic born right here in the lifeblood of East London. Few galleries have so elevated street art to fine art like Nelly. It makes you think in collector's terms about drip-flawed graffiti and bathroom-wall scrawl, encouraging its roster of artists to more complex techniques and more profound themes. Artists who started here have gone on to contribute to shows at Somerset House, MoMA and the V&A.

21 One Good Deed Today
73 Kingsland Road E2
020 7739 9951
onegooddeedtoday.com
Fri–Sat 10–7, Sun 12–5

This shop is located on an unsuspecting stretch only a few minutes from the beating heart of Shoreditch. Everyday sundries are sold from producers who take their material and social impact seriously, the message being that style doesn't need to be comprised by ethics. This place is strong on style, embracing the current appetite for pastels, pattern and succulents, helped along with coffee and doughnuts.

22 Pitfield London
31–35 Pitfield Street N1 6HB
020 7490 6852
pitfieldlondon.com
Daily 10–7

Part Helsinki chic, part Palm Beach, Pitfield is like a faraway haven of Pop Art fabrics, art deco-style room dividers and insane orange leather armchairs from the 1960s. A tea shop serving brownies, meringues and free-range chicken pies occupies the north end of the shop, but what truly distinguishes Pitfield is its roster of exhibitions by independent designers of all walks, from the 'Helsinki' (Klaus Haapaniemi) to the 'Palm Beach' (Jade Jagger). That and Pitfield's obvious respect for interesting pottery by Camille Flammarion and iittala.

23 Ryantown
126 Columbia Road E2 7RG
020 7613 1510
robryanstudio.com
Sat 12–6, Sun 10–4

His aesthetic has so distinctively encapsulated London's craving for the handmade that it's hard to imagine a world without Rob Ryan's paper-cut masterworks. And his shop on Columbia Road is where the artist's cast of cut-out characters comes to roost in uplifting scenes right out of Hans Christian Andersen or Grimms' fairy tales. Ryan's true craft is his artwork, expertly carved out into positive or negative space, as if by a laser, in his studio around the corner. He's not above greeting cards, coffee mugs or wall stickers – he practically invented the genre. And his limited-edition prints are also justifiably popular.

Contemporary concept store Monologue

Bright light
Lee Broom

When he was growing up, designer and entrepreneur Lee Broom aspired to be an actor. At 17 he won a fashion design competition, where he met (and subsequently worked for) Vivienne Westwood. Then came a stint studying fashion design at Central Saint Martins. Following graduation – and almost by mistake – Broom got into designing bar interiors and set up the company Makilee with a friend to undertake such projects. In 2007 he launched his own brand with a focus on designing and manufacturing furniture and products. He has been on a progressive trajectory ever since, opening his own retail space in 2013.

How have things changed since you launched your own brand in 2007?
I designed my debut collection with no restrictions and I really enjoyed that freedom. In 2010, I opened the design studio in Shoreditch during the London Design Festival. I approached the business rather like a fashion brand, starting with couture and then introducing a diffusion collection, which enabled more people to own a piece. We launched the Crystal Bulb in 2012 in Milan, and that was a kind of coming of age. I'd say my designs are less decorative now and more sculptural. My style will continue to evolve. I don't want to become known for one thing.

What made you turn your studio into a shop in 2013?
Prior to that, the studio was also operating as a showroom to display our pieces to architects and dealers. It seemed logical to open as a store for the public as well. It's useful to gauge reactions to our pieces and it's really satisfying to sell directly to our end user.

How has Shoreditch changed since you've been here?
People complain about gentrification, which I understand, but isn't that just what happens in cities? Rivington Street is still developing and, right now, has a good balance of the rough and the smooth.

How would you describe your work to someone who has never seen it?
Traditional yet modern. Fun yet formal. I like to distort the familiar and exaggerate details. My work isn't utilitarian – I like to experiment with luxury. **MF**

15 **Lee Broom**
Electra House, 95 Rivington Street EC2A 3AY
(See page 145)

24 SCP East
135 Curtain Road EC2A 3BX
020 7739 1869
scp.co.uk
Mon-Sat 9.30-6, Sun 11-5

You'd think Sheridan Coakley had done enough, making contemporary British design desirable; helping build careers for local luminaries like Matthew Hilton; sustaining British manufacturing; and reviving a once forgotten corner of East London. He manages to keep a helpful and informative staff, too, at this flagship three-level store in Shoreditch. You can comb the tables for hours, flipping through books, fingering cushions and inspecting pottery. Or wallow in the big-ticket items: vast, inviting sofas, Kay + Stemmer's impossibly smooth shelving and Donna Wilson's furniture range.
(See pages 154–155)

25 Squint
178 Shoreditch High Street E1 6HU
020 7739 9275
squintlimited.com
Mon-Fri 10-6, Sun 1-5

See page 27 for Chelsea shop and further information.

26 Tokyobike
87–89 Tabernacle Street EC2A 4BA
020 7251 6842
tokyobike.co.uk
Tues-Fri 11-7, Sat-Sun 11-5

For a shop that prides itself on its small stature and indie status, there was a lot of fanfare when Tokyobike opened in 2012. But then a Tokyobike is not just a comfortable ride, it's also seriously chic. As if to drive home the point, the Shoreditch showroom has the builder's-white walls and reclaimed floors of a gallery, with slender cycles in candy colours around the perimeter and low displays of Japanese- and British-designed homewares directing the flow. Tokyobike staff are Japanese imports too, bike buffs of the smartly dressed sort you rarely see in the London shops.

Sweet success
Rick & Michael Mast,
Mast Brothers

Strolling along Redchurch Street, you'd be forgiven for mistaking Mast Brothers for an art gallery: the slick glass frontage; the neon sign; the artfully arranged hessian sacks of cocoa beans; the clean-lined interior. Yet enter their domain and the aroma hanging in the air implies only one thing: chocolate.

For centuries, people have marvelled at the nuances imparted in wine. More recently, coffee has undergone such expert scrutiny and we've all turned into overnight aficionados. So could the opening of Mast Brothers' London store signal the same worshipping of the cocoa bean?

Rick and Michael Mast, who grew up in the American Midwest state of Iowa, set up their chocolate business in 2007 with a desire to explore one of mankind's greatest pleasures. Some would say they're at the pinnacle of the craft chocolate movement and are most certainly embedded in the US bean-to-bar maker scene.

Based in Williamsburg, a hipster Brooklyn hub where most things are dubbed 'artisan', the duo have built a solid following and sell their bars across the country, and the world. With a keen eye on London and an appreciation for the characteristics of Shoreditch, they bagged a prime spot on Redchurch Street to make and sell their chocolate creations.

It is with pride that the bearded brothers show us behind the scenes, acknowledging their fellow bearded colleagues as they go. We're sipping their very own chocolate beer – a pleasant non-alcoholic fizzy beverage that tastes very different to what you might expect. Visible from the shop space, behind an internal glass wall, all sorts of processes unfold: husking, chipping, grinding, blending, aging, tempering, pouring... Thankfully, they run regular tours to explain it all.

Waiting for you in the main shop – the contemporary temple for chocolate lovers – are perfect stacks of beautifully packaged bars together with tasting notes. Each flavour – be it vanilla & smoke, almond, maple, sea salt, black truffle, chilli pepper or single origin – has its own graphic wrap, successfully luring in anyone with an appreciation of fine packaging, if not its contents. Purists will be drawn to the glass cabinet displaying perfect cubes of chocolate truffle; the various drinks on offer may seduce everyone else. **MF**

38 **Mast Brothers**
19–29 Redchurch Street E2 7DJ
(See page 156)

27 Tord Boontje Shop
23 Charlotte Road EC2A 3PB
020 7717 5398
shop.tordboontje.com
Tues–Sat 11–6

Tord Boontje opened his loft-showroom in 2012 and immediately launched the basement space as a gallery for collaborations with designers big (Swarovski) and small (Tracey Neuls). His Garland lights, created for Habitat more than 10 years ago, and their successors, Icarus and Midsummer, will always be the top sellers on this well-trodden stretch of Charlotte Road, but he's constantly on the go, leaving no home accessory unturned – each season brings a new range of glassware, tableware or jewellery, alongside T-shirts, stationery and table mats.

28 Tracey Neuls
73 Redchurch Street E2 7DJ
020 7018 0872
traceyneuls.com
Tues–Sun 11–6

See page 63 for Marylebone shop and further information, and pages 58–63 for interview.

29 Two Columbia Road
2 Columbia Road E2 7NN
020 7729 9933
twocolumbiaroad.com
Wed–Fri 12–7, Sat 11–5, Sun 10–4

Keith Roberts' lifeblood is vintage: serious, quality, top-of-its-game vintage that plays for our appetite for rosewood sideboards and vast, clean-lined seating. Not everything has a prestige designer attached to it – though Roberts manages to get his hands on a steady stream of Vodders and Wegners, among other Euro heavyweights – but those that don't will have lots in common with the popular midcentury schools. Two Columbia does have a sense of humour, though, and it comes out in the accessories: cocky plastic table lamps from Atari era, for instance, and wood-burning stoves from swingin' 1960s chalets.

30 Unto This Last
230 Brick Lane E2 7EB
020 7613 0882
untothislast.co.uk
Daily 10–6

There's no mistaking an Unto This Last product. The craftsmanship is flawless, the output is all bespoke, yet the prices are affordable. Unto This Last eschews the factory, warehouse and logistics of mass manufacturers by using high-tech equipment and uniform materials to produce its furniture expediently and, most vitally, cheaply. No packaging, no distribution and a minuscule supply chain mean the designers can do all their handiwork at this Brick Lane showroom-atelier – behind a wall of glass that gives it an almost 'while-u-wait' atmosphere (though lead times are realistically a couple of weeks).

31 YCN
72 Rivington Street EC2A 3AY
020 7033 2140
ycn.org
Mon–Fri 10–6, Sat–Sun 11–4

The Young Creative Network has always aspired to do more than it says on the tin. It got into the game of representing talent, then branched out to run its own creative agency. And several years ago it opened this gallery-shop to exhibit and sell the work of its more bankable members, work that extends to prints, maps, wrapping paper, wallpaper, scarves, and cards. The interior, designed by London's Klassnik Corporation, is a thing of beauty itself. Its mobile vitrines and shelves fit back into the woodwork like pieces in a puzzle. The décor is as much a draw as the roster of art installations and the small but perfectly formed lending library.

PECO MATCH
THREE STEAMERS
SAFETY MATCHES
DO NOT GLOW
Primus

Prime mover

Sheridan Coakley, *SCP*

Sheridan Coakley is one of Shoreditch's pioneers, having settled in Curtain Road when the area was 'a black hole outside the City', long before the 1990s East London boom. His company, SCP, was also one of London's first contemporary furniture manufacturers and retailers, collaborating early on with Matthew Hilton, Jasper Morrison and Terence Woodgate. In 2015, SCP celebrated 30 years in business.

What led you to Shoreditch and what was the state of the neighbourhood when you arrived?
In the early 1980s I was dealing in vintage furniture, mostly 1930s modernist tubular-steel, and I found a company in Rivington Street that rechromed furniture. I was coming backwards and forwards into what was a desolate area. By that time, any furniture business that had survived the war had moved out into a sensible factory on one floor. But Hackney Council wouldn't allow any change of use. Then a few brave people thought, 'To hell with it, I'm just going to move in.'

It reminded me of SoHo, New York, in the 1970s. People moved in illegally, lots of artists. I saw this empty place that was incredibly cheap and rented the main floor. Eventually the council relaxed the zoning, which moved Shoreditch on to a different level.

I did an exhibition of Philippe Starck's furniture for Baleri. I'd already met people like Jasper and Matthew when I ran a tiny shop in Notting Hill, and they were producing steel furniture in a similar style. I used that company around the corner to manufacture some of their designs. My only customers were designers and architects, because they were at the vanguard of that change. It wasn't until the late 1990s that I felt confident enough to change this into a shop.

What do you think drove the British acceptance of modern furniture?
I think the country gradually woke up to the modern world and the awareness that we should be creating things. We had no industry left. But we were good at being creative.

Eventually SCP became synonymous with honest British manufacturing. How did that happen?
We were first port of call. I did Konstantin Grcic's first pieces because there weren't many companies like mine around. Italy had dominated the furniture business, but Britain's always been good at coming up in a maverick, independent way with new trends, and I think that played a part of it.

Has Shoreditch changed too much for your liking?
It's got a long way to go before it becomes another Covent Garden and I feel I need to move out. What's good is that people live and work in the area and it's a destination. There are still lots of empty spaces, which will, hopefully, turn into interesting things.

Who are the 'new guard' of SCP designers?
Lucy Kurrein – we're working on our third product with her. Reiko Kaneko, the ceramicist, has designed a very interesting armchair that we're going to try to make – it's nice to get designers out of their comfort zone. We're also launching some new textiles with a young designer called Hannah Waldron.

Anything you would never carry?
I used to say cushions. But now we sell thousands. EH

24 **SCP East** 135 Curtain Road EC2A 3BX
(See page 150)

For anything
32 Boundary
2–4 Boundary Street E2 7DD
020 7729 1051
theboundary.co.uk

Enjoy moreish pastries from their Albion bakery next door, proper French cooking in the dining room, or an alcoholic booster on the rooftop.

For pretty dinner
33 The Clove Club
Shoreditch Town Hall
380 Old Street EC1V 9LT
020 7729 6496
thecloveclub.com

This was recently issued with a Michelin star for its thoughtful approach to seasonal, British cooking. Its sports a sparse interior with pretty navy-tiled open kitchen, punchy cocktails, and knowledgeable staff.

For posh pub grub
34 The Culpeper
40 Commercial Street E1 6LP
020 7247 5371
theculpeper.com

A beautifully refurbished tavern with high ceilings and a striking geometrical metal sculpture doubling up as the bar. The stunning menu features locally grown ingredients.

For buzzing breakfast
35 Dishoom
7 Boundary Street E2 7JE
020 7420 9324
dishoom.com

Kick into your day at this buzzing Bombay-style cafe with an egg naan roll and the wondrous house chai.

For brunch-tails
36 Hoi Polloi
100 Shoreditch High Street E1 6JQ
020 8880 6100
hoi-polloi.co.uk

Hipster wood-panelled hotel bar where you can dabble in Bibi Spritzes with brunch from midday–6pm – try the hot smoked salmon hash – or stick around for Aunt Nell's Espresso Martinis.

For sunny lunch
37 Lyle's
Tea Building
56 Shoreditch High Street E1 6JJ
020 3019 2468
lyleslondon.com

Largely white and grey restaurant where, if sunny, there is no lovelier or more elegant place to have lunch, especially one cooked by James Rowe, one of London's best up-and-coming chefs.

For smart chocolate
38 Mast Brothers
Unit 2, 19–29 Redchurch Street
E2 7DJ
020 7739 1236
mastbrothers.com

This New York import, run by two brothers, is sparse, with central pedestals for displaying supreme bars of graphically packaged chocolate – a bit like the sweet version of an Apple Store. (See pages 150–152)

For gratifying dinner
39 Merchants Tavern
36 Charlotte Road EC2A 3PG
020 7060 5335
merchantstavern.co.uk

Inside this former Victorian warehouse, chefs Angela Hartnett and Neil Borthwick boast sumptuous design, intelligent cooking, an enjoyable soundtrack, and charming staff.

For cool coffee
40 Ozone
11 Leonard Street EC2A 4AQ
020 7490 1039
ozonecoffee.co.uk

Pleasingly designed coffee shop with tall brick and sand coloured walls, brushed wood, kooky coffee photography, and bubbly staff who can take you through the long menu.

Below, Merchants Tavern boasts sumptuous design

Right, hipster hangout Hoi Polloi at the Ace Hotel

For Portuguese lunch

41 Taberna do Mercado
107B Commercial Street E1 6BG
tabernamercado.co.uk

Nuno Mendes may have earned a star in his more glamorous former posts, but the food here, served on pretty china, sings of his Portuguese homeland. Order a pork bifana sandwich.

BOOK A ROOM

For constant creativity

42 Ace Hotel London Shoreditch
100 Shoreditch High Street E1 6JQ
020 7613 9800
acehotel.com/london

For Conran cool

43 Boundary
2–4 Boundary Street E2 7DD
020 7729 1051
theboundary.co.uk

London's hotels are ever-changing. Hoteliers know that it takes more than just a comfy bed to make discerning travellers dream. Exemplary service and distinctive design are everything. Globetrotters prefer a buzzing bar over a dowdy dining room. They opt for speedy Wi-Fi over an incompatible Hi-Fi. They expect a clued-up concierge over a dozy doorman. Never ones to stand still, London's hotels are putting the 'hot' into hotel, explains **Lauren Ho**

With some 18 million visitors hitting the British capital each year, London consistently tops the list as one of the most frequented cities in the world. A central hub for international travel, Heathrow airport services a whopping 70 million passengers annually, fuelling an industry that is worth approximately £13billion. And despite global economic uncertainty in recent times, this weighty influx of tourists is increasing year on year, prompting the all-important question of where to bed down.

With over 1,000 hotels on offer, the competition between hoteliers has turned into all-out warfare as they vie for differentiation and make a play for that prized check-in. For many holidaymakers, when it comes to picking a hotel, good design, architecture and access to technology is now paramount, with a new generation of traveller expecting more in the way of affordable luxury and fast service, single-handedly changing the dynamics of the travel market. Backpackers no longer need to endure bog-standard lodgings, as a new breed of hip hostels such as Freehand, the low-cost option from the group behind New York's NoMad hotel, and Generator shape the industry with innovative design, instant service, superior technology and a range of sleeping options that include dormitories and more private double rooms, catering to all types of guests. CitizenM, the inexpensive brand that started life a decade ago in Amsterdam, has also built a reputation for providing luxury for less. Its second outpost in London is no different. Located in the city's now-buzzing Bankside area, a short stroll from the Tate Modern, the hotel provides a no-frills offering from manual check-in counters on arrival, to a self-service canteen, making way for the more important necessities, such as top-notch design and free Wi-Fi and movies. And, they say, "absolutely no trouser presses, bellboys, or stupid pillow chocolates". Of course, what happens in London sets the precedent for elsewhere. Take India, for example, where the country's swish Park Hotel brand has recently extended to include Zone by the Park Hotels, a new type of trendy, affordable accommodation for the growing number of domestic travellers.

Premier room,
Rosewood London,
Holborn
(see page 103)

Left to right, suite with terrace and deluxe room at The London EDITION, Fitzrovia (page 67); seventh floor terrace (top) and deluxe double room (bottom) at Ace Hotel London Shoreditch (page 157)

With the demand for outstanding design at an all-time high, even the industry's traditional brands have jumped on the bandwagon, shaking up their once staid outlook. Indeed, the somewhat conventional Marriott International launched its lifestyle arm with The London EDITION. The brainchild of hospitality legend Ian Schrager, the hotel follows his failsafe formula and centres around a buzzing destination lobby. With outposts in Miami and New York, as well as six more in the pipeline, it seems inevitable that hoteliers should come up with a contemporary solution that satisfies consumer needs.

This rise of the 'Millennials' or 'Generation Y' has also remodelled the way hotels interact with the outside world, compelling them to raise their game, focusing on an online presence and social networking. Brands like the Ace and Hoxton hotels have gone one step further, integrating their lobbies into social workspaces, offering free Wi-Fi and turning the hotel into a hangout – a traditional Stateside concept that has started to take root in a more sophisticated version in London; hotels such as Mondrian and The Beaumont, the debut hotel from restaurant legends Corbin & King, have included the local community in their business plans, prioritising public access to their restaurants, bars and spas, resulting in hotels becoming hotspot destinations.

London might be at the forefront of industry trends, but it is the city's quintessential Grande Dame hotels, such as the Ritz, Claridge's and the Dorchester – most of which have been comprehensively restored – that are on better form than ever. Retaining the character that defined them when they first opened their doors during Victorian or Edwardian times, these hotels encapsulate afternoon tea, charming service and opulent interiors, and are partly responsible for establishing the benchmark for major international players to set up shop in

Left to right, entrance gallery and premier suite at Rosewood London, Holborn (page 103); lobby at CitizenM, Southwark (page 193)

extraordinary sites; both Shangri-La (in the Shard) and Rosewood Hotels (in a grand 1914 Belle Époque building) have made an inaugural appearance within recent years. Next up, Canadian brand Four Seasons will launch a much-anticipated third hotel in the Grade II-listed 10 Trinity Square.

Of course, the arrival of the so-called 'sharing economy' has had a major impact on the demand for hotels, as different cities grapple with adapting to the emergence of short-term apartment rental companies like Airbnb. Barcelona's response was to fine the company for breaching local tourism regulations, while London's plan to overturn a 40-year old law banning short-term rentals has had a mixed reaction. However, like all new concepts, this too has its pros and cons, depending on the demographic. Rather than a threat, this is an extension of the ever-evolving hospitality world that, if embraced, can positively alter tourism and the demand for hotels. And while it has seemingly unsettled the long-established pattern that has previously dictated the industry, no doubt it will bounce back, prove its resilience and stoically adapt to consumer needs.

London is one of the few cities that travellers can visit time and again and continue to be surprised. Expansive parks, free museums and iconic sites such as Big Ben and the Tower of London mean it will always be a natural tourist attraction, but it's the frenetic melting pot of cultures that has defined the true heart of the city. From fashion and design to art and architecture, everything that modern London stands for, has uniquely developed to find a means of representing all corners of society. There are no set rules, which is precisely what has shaped the hospitality industry into the success it is today.

Lauren Ho is a luxury design and travel writer, consultant and the travel editor at *Wallpaper**. She writes for various hotel magazines, including the Four Seasons, Mandarin Oriental and the Maybourne Hotel Group.

HACKNEY

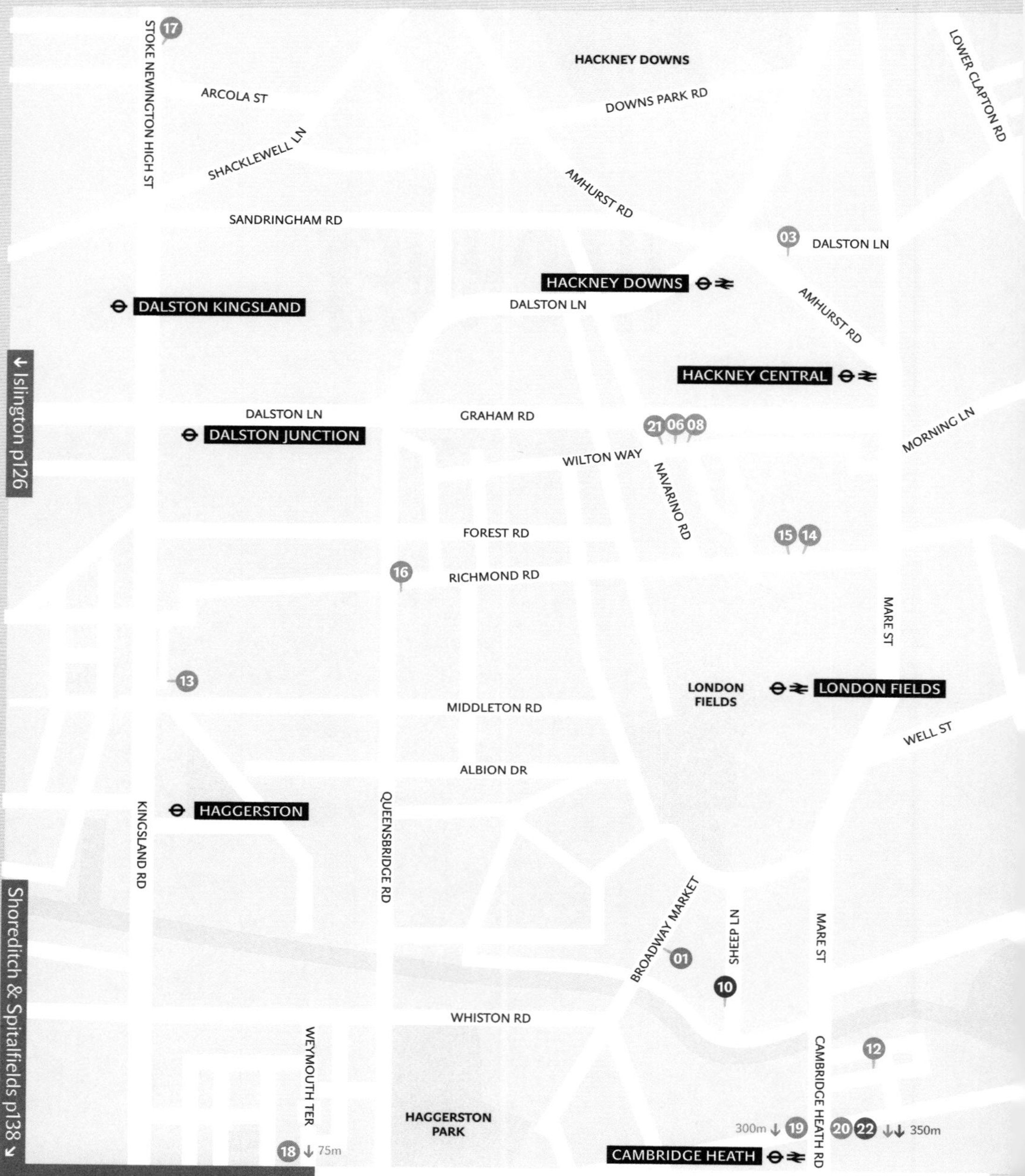

HACKNEY DOWNS
DOWNS PARK RD
LOWER CLAPTON RD
STOKE NEWINGTON HIGH ST
ARCOLA ST
SHACKLEWELL LN
AMHURST RD
SANDRINGHAM RD
DALSTON LN
HACKNEY DOWNS
DALSTON KINGSLAND
DALSTON LN
AMHURST RD
HACKNEY CENTRAL
← Islington p126
DALSTON LN
DALSTON JUNCTION
GRAHAM RD
WILTON WAY
MORNING LN
NAVARINO RD
FOREST RD
RICHMOND RD
MARE ST
LONDON FIELDS
LONDON FIELDS
MIDDLETON RD
WELL ST
ALBION DR
HAGGERSTON
KINGSLAND RD
QUEENSBRIDGE RD
Shoreditch & Spitalfields p138 ↘
BROADWAY MARKET
SHEEP LN
MARE ST
WHISTON RD
WEYMOUTH TER
HAGGERSTON PARK
CAMBRIDGE HEATH RD
300m ↓
↓↓ 350m
↓ 75m
CAMBRIDGE HEATH
17 03 21 06 08 15 14 16 13 01 10 12 19 20 22 18

Design galleries & institutions
Design shops & C20th vintage
Design bookshops
Eat, drink & sleep (pages 176–177)

01 Artwords Bookshop
02 Béton Brut
03 Chase & Sorensen
04 Everything But The Dog
05 Haus
06 J. Glinert
07 The Modern Warehouse
08 Momosan
09 The Peanut Vendor
10 Rocket
11 Triangle

Hackney

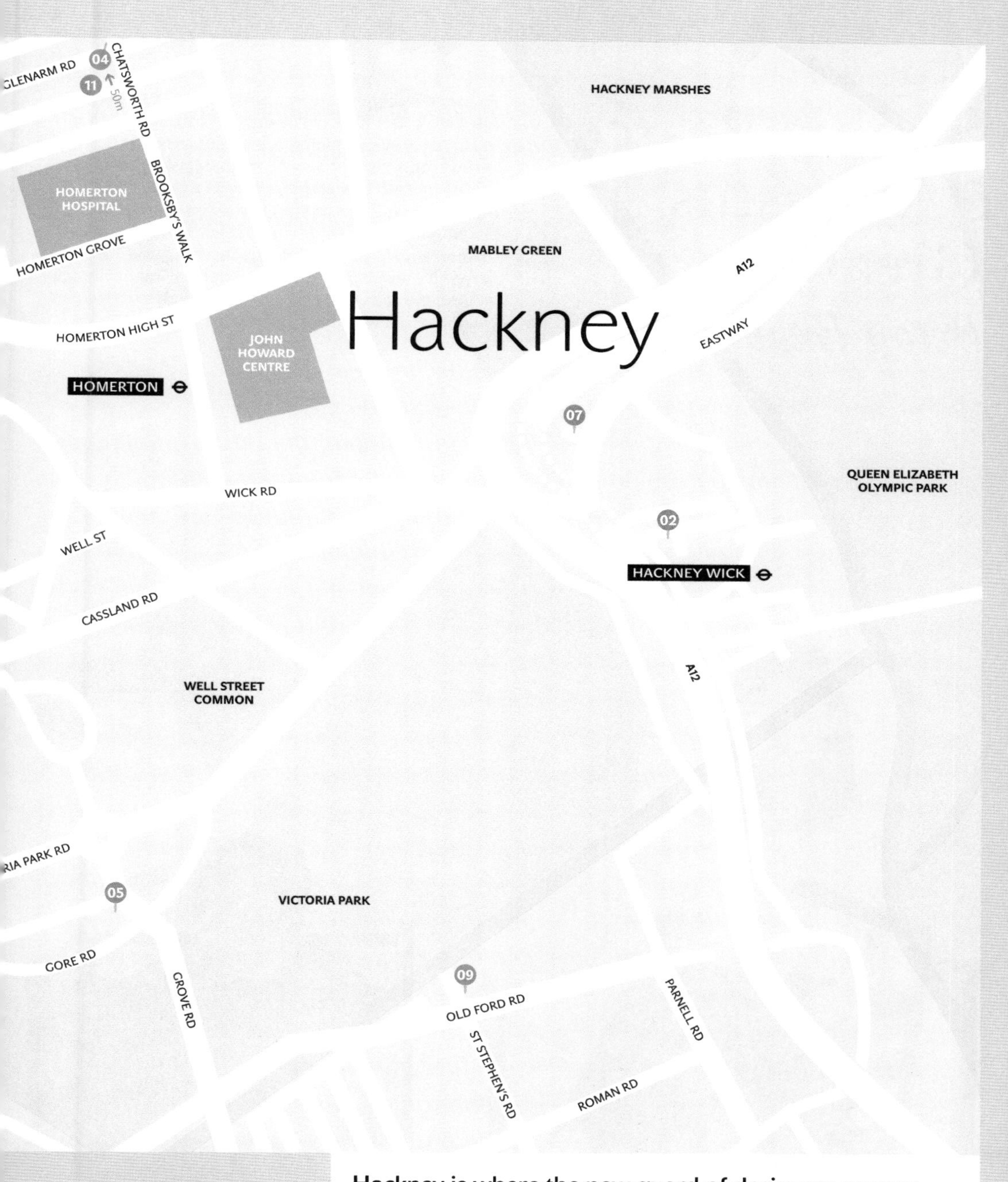

Hackney is where the new guard of designers occupy studios and shoebox shops. The heart is London Fields, where weekend warriors come to barbecue on the grass or devour pulled-pork sandwiches from Broadway Market. Wandering aimlessly can be daunting but never boring, this being a breeding ground for fashion trends. A foodie mecca has sprung up around Lower Clapton, but the décor – human or otherwise – is the thing.

Brut force
Sophie Pearce & Augustus Greaves
Béton Brut

Founded by Sophie Pearce and Augustus Greaves in April 2015, Béton Brut is a design store and gallery in Hackney Wick, joining a greater concentration of 20th-century design dealers in East London. Pearce traded in a job as a charity PR with a background in political journalism to start her online vintage store, Osi Modern, in 2010. Augustus, scion of the English furniture-makers Greaves and Thomas, gave up carpentry and building work to deal in Dutch vintage around the same time. They met as rivals but decided collaboration was the way forward.

How was it that the two of you came to launch Béton Brut in the first place?
We met at an exhibition called Designjunction in 2013, as rival dealers and exhibitors. Our pieces sat so well together that some mistook one stand for the other. Post-show debriefs soon turned into Hackney bike rides scouting for empty premises and talks of a merger.

What sort of 20th century pieces are you particularly keen on sourcing?
Béton Brut sources interesting, seminal and rare design from across Europe. We call the collection 'architect-led' because a majority of the pieces were designed by an architect – Alvar Aalto, Martin Visser, Friso Kramer and Superstudio to name a few.

Your selection favours Dutch modernism. Why?
Unlike Scandinavian design, which has seen a great resurgence in recent years, Dutch modern design is still a well-kept secret. Béton Brut is one of only a handful of dealers bringing it to the UK. But we don't expect it to stay a secret for very long. Dutch design was concerned with the principle of '*Goed Wonen*' (good living) a post-war ideal professing that simple, affordable and well-designed interiors would make people freer and happier. Think stripped back minimalism, grounded in function, but a bit more fun. A brave new world of colourful metal, bent plywood and sculptural forms.

What words would you use to describe Béton Brut?
Minimalist, architectural, sculptural, seminal.

You've opened your store in Hackney Wick. Why did you choose this area?
We chose Hackney Wick for its vibrancy and cultural interest. There are so many artists and creative businesses operating behind warehouse doors, and thriving bars and pop-ups, but not many shops as yet. It also afforded us more space – the pieces really have a chance to breathe in a large gallery-like setting.

What are some of the other services you offer?
We offer reupholstery, sourcing and design services. We can come to your house or premises and suggest what pieces might work, as well as have any seating redone with bespoke upholstery to match the scheme. For the trade, our space is also evolving as a prop-hire studio and location for shoots.

Where does the name Béton Brut come from?
'Béton Brut' – meaning 'raw concrete' – was a concrete finish coined by Le Corbusier and used in modernist architecture. It can be seen at the Southbank and the Hayward Gallery. It is honest and uncompromising, just like the collection. **MF**

02 **Béton Brut**
Unit 2, 30 Felstead Street E9 5LG
(see right)

01 **Artwords Bookshop**
20–22 Broadway Market E8 4QJ
020 7923 7507
artwords.co.uk
Mon–Fri 10.30–8, Sat–Sun 10–6

This is where rail-thin Hackney creatives nourish themselves with weighty tomes on contemporary German photorealists of the 1970s or peek furtively at photo-tributes to Jeff Koons. Its speciality is contemporary art and design, which extends to graphic novels, videos, magazines and special editions. Authors and artists often hold events and signings here, packing the stark white space to capacity. (See page 139 for Shoreditch shop)

02 **Béton Brut**
Unit 2, 30 Felstead Street E9 5LG
020 7018 1890
betonbrut.co.uk
Sat 11–5 and Mon–Fri by appointment

Occupying a sizeable, clean, bright space in an unsuspecting new build, Béton Brut's friendly and knowledgeable owners (see left) treat furniture and lighting as functional art. Pieces from varying decades sit side by side – early 1930s bentwood chairs by Finnish designer Alvar Aalto nestle alongside postmodern statement desks from the 1970s by Superstudio – unified by a singular architectural aesthetic.

03 **Chase & Sorensen**
238B Dalston Lane E8 1LQ
020 8533 5523
chaseandsorensen.com
Tues–Sat 10–6, Thurs 10–7, Sun 12–6

Dane Signe Sorensen and her partner Brent Chase source Danish modern goodies via a reliable network on the ground in Denmark. These aren't flawless specimens from banks and opera houses, rather pretty, homely midcentury pieces that create that familiar Scandi look just as effectively. If you've never lived with Danish modern, visit the showroom on the fringes of Dalston, where you can try before you buy.

セロテープ
Metropolitan
Metropolitan

A Hackney stroll with
Tom Budding, *J. Glinert*

Enter J. Glinert, Tom Budding's small shop on Wilton Way (see page 172), and it's hard to miss the selection of books dedicated to the architectural history of Hackney. Chatting to Budding, who was born and bred there, his passion for the area is palpable. It only seems right to ask him to take us on a quick tour around some of his favourite local places.

Locking up his shop, we set off along Wilton Way, a quiet street that has changed considerably over the past few years. He points out his neighbour's homeware shop **Momosan** (see page 172) and new restaurant **Pidgin** across the road, at which point I ask him how the locals received his shop when it opened in 2012. "The shop was well received," he claims, "except for a few leftwing types moaning about us turning up with our 'flash little bits'. They shop here now," he jokes.

We head up the road to the back of **Hackney Town Hall**, turning onto the quiet pedestrianised Sylvester Path, once the main street that connected Hackney to the City. Reaching busy Mare Street, we survey the scene standing outside the **Cock Tavern**, a pub that used to be a bit dodgy but has recently been 'gastrofied.' What does he make of the rapid gentrification of Hackney? Surprisingly for a lifelong resident, he has no problem with it and sees it as inevitable progress. He welcomes the area becoming safer and shaking its rough image.

Crossing over Mare Street, a rarity for Budding, we head along Morning Lane and turn into Belsham Street to admire the sensitively converted warehouse space that is now the studio of designer Martino Gamper and his artist partner Francis Upritchard. Its location is quite unique, sandwiched between derelict buildings, a Tesco superstore and ugly tower blocks across the road, and several flashy discount fashion outlets in neighbouring streets including Burberry, Pringle and Aquascutum. Budding laughs at the flurry of foreign shoppers, often walking

J. Glinert

Momosan

Martino Gamper's studio

Lennox House

Rawduck

Choosing Keeping

around looking somewhat lost. "If you set up a Parisian cake shop on Mare Street, it would be out of control," he suggests. More outlets are set to open behind Tesco, once the renovation of the railway arches is complete.

As we wind through back streets, Budding raves about our next stop – **Lennox House** on Cresset Road. The residential building was originally built in 1937 to designs by John Eric Miers Macgregor and is considered to be one of the finest examples of social housing in London. The stepped sections give every flat a private balcony and plenty of natural light. The building's central space was originally intended to house a market to help subsidise the rents, and the design was a precursor for the larger Brunswick Centre, built in the 1960s.

Snaking back to Mare Street along Loddiges Road and a sea of council houses, Budding talks enthusiastically about **Loddiges Nursery**, which was located on this land during the 18th and 19th centuries. The Nursery was the largest hothouse in Britain and traded in exotic plants when Hackney was still a suburban village.

Heading back to his shop, we pass one of his favourite restaurants, **Rawduck**, on Richmond Road. We chat about the endless stream of cool new bars, restaurants, boutiques and niche offerings flowing into Hackney. He embraces their arrival, although he quips, "When I get tired of cool places, I go where the old ladies go."

Hopping into his car, we head to Columbia Road to visit **Choosing Keeping**, a small shop selling a selection of exquisite stationery and other specially sourced tabletop items. Owner Julia, aka 'The Pen Lady' to Budding, joins us for a quick caffeine hit around the corner on Hackney Road at the unassuming **Lanark** coffee shop.

Prior to leaving, we head down some stairs and discover the world of designer and maker **Dean Edmonds**, who has his workshop below. Here he makes bespoke functionalist furniture and products, including a simple three-pronged coat hook sold at J. Glinert. Budding is clearly animated by the existence of a local workshop and is proud to be selling some of its output. He envisages selling more of his own creations in the future, made by specialists here and across Europe.

In the few hours spent with him, one thing seems very clear: Budding has a happy-go-lucky attitude, allowing his inquisitive mind to constantly open new doors to fresh influences. Speaking of opening doors, after an enjoyable few hours in the afternoon sun, he heads back to Wilton Way ready to welcome more customers into his world. **MF**

Right, Budding's homeware store J. Glinert

HACKNEY HOUSES
FROM TOWER TO TOWER BLOCK
KINFOLK
MONOCLE
HACKNEY HOUSES

04 Everything But The Dog
65 Chatsworth Road E5 0LH
07414 99 1228
everythingbutthedog.eu
Wed–Sat 11–7, Sun 12–5

You're likely to encounter the dog in question as soon as you step over the threshold of this tiny, new shop on the ever-changing Chatsworth Road. As the name suggests, everything else in store is for sale and reasonably priced, including copper cocktail mugs, durable school tumblers, tactile oak cheese plates and a changing array of vintage furniture. Much of it is by Ercol, but there are also midcentury items such as cabinets, shelving and other pieces found on the owners' travels.

05 Haus
39 Morpeth Road E9 7LD
020 8533 8024
hauslondon.com
Thurs–Sat 11–6, Sun 11–5

A design shop with the heft of a central London purveyor but none of the attitude, Haus is run by Jane and Andrew Tye, who manage to show an impressive amount in their tight corner plot. A sculptor and designer respectively, the couple are well versed in what will please and last. With that in mind, they support a balance of practical Scandinavians (Muuto, Hay) and Europeans (Vitra, Magis), with an occasional nod to green producers like Hampson Woods, who make chopping boards from trees felled in Russell Square. They also carry a canny selection of pendant lighting.

06 J. Glinert
71 Wilton Way E8 1BG
020 7249 6815
jglinert.com
Thurs–Sat 11–6, Sun 12–5

This tiny shop on tranquil Wilton Way is run by Tom Budding, a man who is so passionate about everything he sells, you'd be mad not to engage in conversation with him on a visit. Here he aims to sell hardware, office and household items that you can't find elsewhere. Utilitarian products prevail, including paper clips, brushes, toolboxes, hair combs, Japanese adhesive tape, chopping boards, lightbulbs… you name it. Various publications about Hackney adorn the shelves – get Budding started on the subject and you'll enjoy many a historical fact. (See pages 168–171)

07 The Modern Warehouse
3 Trafalgar Mews E9 5JG
020 8986 0740
themodernwarehouse.com
Sat 11–5, or by appointment

You can't honestly call yourself a Scandinavian furniture buff until you've pored over the stock at Rob McClymont and David Tatham's warehouse. The partners got into importing back when it was a very lonely game. The market has since exploded, but The Modern Warehouse's suppliers are steadfast and the logistics unchanged. Hans Wegner fans will not go hungry here: he is the rule not the exception. There are also armies of leather-backed teak chairs by Finn Juhl, firm wool Bjorn Jorgensen sofas and two-tone armchairs by Ejner Larsen and Aksel Bender Madsen.

08 Momosan
79a Wilton Way E8 1BG
020 7249 4989
momosanshop.com
Thurs–Sun 11–6

Momoko Mizutani has lived in Japan and the UK and as such chooses items to sell in her shop that reflect her experiences of both. This is the place to find teapots, brass trivets and wooden bowls from Japan alongside pottery, stools and jewellery by British designers such as Martino Gamper, Gemma Holt and Max Lamb. Displays are clear and simple in this bright space, which feels comforting and calm, as is the service should you have any questions. Keep an eye out for changing window displays, often dedicated to a different artist or designer.

10 The Peanut Vendor
6 Gunmakers Lane E3 5GG
020 8981 8613
thepeanutvendor.co.uk
Mon-Fri 8-6, Sat 9.30-6, Sun 10-6

The Peanut Vendor recently moved from Newington Green to these larger modern premises near the canal by Victoria Park. Stock here is honest and well sourced, ticking a checklist of early- to mid-20th-century British, Danish and French teak and rosewood classics. Odd tin signage and handwoven textiles give personality to the place, as do the owners, Barny and Becky, whose life's work is market-hopping for quality bargains. There's also a cafe.

10 Rocket
4-6 Sheep Lane E8 4QS
020 7254 8391
rocketgallery.com
Daily 11-6

Rocket's owner Jonathan Stephenson moved his gallery from Shoreditch to this hidden spot behind Broadway Market and converted the space into his dream gallery and studio. The ultra-modern combination of concrete structure and bright white lighting provides the perfect environment for Stephenson's geometrical minimalist art, as well as furniture by Jens Risom, photo books by Martin Parr and rugs by fashion designer Jonathan Saunders. (See pages 174–175)

11 Triangle
92A Chatsworth Road E5 0LH
020 8510 9361
trianglestore.co.uk
Thurs-Sun 11-6

Three close friends, Tori Mullen, Mary Wagstaff and Matthew Naylor, founded Triangle on the increasingly cool Chatsworth Road. This two-level store features a carefully curated selection of homewares, accessories, books and stationery that are graphic, often colourful and appropriately functional. Apothecary, bags, watches and jewellery also make up the mix but it is the occasional vintage object or furnishing that helps soften the feeling of newness.

Carefully curated homeware at Clapton's Triangle

Solo visionary
Jonathan Stephenson, *Rocket*

The world of Rocket is one that its founder Jonathan Stephenson has nurtured for over two decades. Stephenson's vision has spawned a 'laboratory' for exploring the crossover of the worlds of art, photography, design and, more recently, fashion. He is a true independent, never happier than discussing the finer details of his unique ventures: book projects with artist Martin Parr, a furniture brand launch with Lars Wolter, limited-edition artists' books with Michelle Grabner, furniture collections with fashion designer Jonathan Saunders. Rocket's ongoing trajectory is unfolding within its new home, a clean-lined, 325-square-metre gallery close to Broadway Market.

You've moved Rocket out of Shoreditch and into London Fields. Why?
It's always good to stay one step ahead and in 20 years of Rocket I've tried to be a pioneer in different areas. It keeps the business fresh and evolving. Firstly in Old Burlington Street (between Savile Row and Cork Street) when the area was half empty after the 1990s recession. Then in Shoreditch, when you couldn't even buy a coffee in the area. Now in London Fields, an area that has been gradually developing for the last 15 years and which has really built up steam in the last two or three. Shoreditch had changed so much, and the gallery had begun to operate as a free museum for the tourists who now flood to the area for hotels, restaurants and clothes shopping. It was no longer a particularly creative area. Furthermore, I wanted to operate in a less public manner and deliberately not have a shopfront. But most importantly, I wanted a bigger space that was suitable for several activities and strands of the business to operate simultaneously.

Have you seen a different kind of customer as a result?
Rocket's client base tends to be international – perhaps 75 per cent of our sales are to clients abroad. Many of our best clients rarely or never visit the premises.

What is different about the new space?
This space has enabled me to have different zones: the main gallery space for art and design exhibitions; the ground floor showroom for furniture or graphics or fashion projects; the design studio for my own book design and typography; and the photography studio for my son Hamish's work and for other photographers and fashion designers to use. It's a totally flexible and creative space.

You've created a comfortable relationship between design and art, both 20th century and contemporary. What are you looking for in the pieces you select?
In design I am a slave to functionality. I am not interested in design as "lifestyle". In both the art and design pieces that I choose to exhibit, I am looking for a minimal, uncluttered aesthetic. Above all, I am searching for clarity: clarity of execution, clarity of message and clarity of function. **MF**

10 Rocket 4–6 Sheep Lane E8 4QS
(See page 173)

For dinner
12 Bistrotheque
23–27 Wadeson Street E2 9DR
020 8983 7900
bistrotheque.com

Expect honest modern European classics in this elegant white loft space set inside a converted clothing factory. Good prix fixe menu for £20. Book ahead.

For posh fried chicken
13 Chick 'n' Sours
390 Kingsland Road E8 4AA
chicknsours.co.uk

Offering an intelligent take on one of the world's favourite comfort foods, former pop-up restaurant chef Carl Clarke fries his chicken using his favourite ingredients from India and South East Asia, washing them down with sour cocktails. The small but gorgeous dining room features blue and white Turkish-inspired floor tiles, half exposed brickwork and a brilliant blue kitchen.

For piggy lunch
14 Lardo
197–201 Richmond Road E8 3NJ
020 8985 2683
lardo.co.uk

This former warehouse houses a wood-fired pizza oven, as well as a rooftop bar and summer barbecue. Order the gorgeous fennel pollen salami and everything on the antipasti menu.

For healthy breakfast
15 Rawduck
197 Richmond Road E8 3NJ
020 8986 6534
rawduckhackney.co.uk

Owned by the team behind the brilliant Ducksoup restaurant in Soho, this incarnation features plenty of concrete, re-hashed wood and refectory tables, and is known for its Japanese-inspired healthy approach to food and drink. Good harissa eggs, as well as an intriguing assortment of ferments and pickles.

For fresh lunch
16 The Richmond
316 Queensbridge Road E8 3NH
020 7241 1638
therichmondhackney.com

This was previously the crazily eccentric LMNT restaurant and before that a pub, but is now a smart dining room and fashion crowd favourite specialising in fish (including a Saturday oyster happy hour) and excellent roasts. Head chef Brett Redman also runs Elliot's in Borough Market.

For intimate drinks
17 Ruby's
76 Stoke Newington Road N16 7XB
020 8211 8690
rubysdalston.com

Shadowy subterranean cocktail bar, found beneath an old cinema sign and run by the modest Tom Gibson, who shakes up brilliant classics and other terrific concoctions, including a Rhubarb Sour and a Chilli Apple Martini.

Opposite, refectory dining at Rawduck

Above, Hackney Road wine bar Sager + Wilde

Eat, drink & sleep

For drinks and cheese

18 Sager + Wilde
193 Hackney Road E2 8JL
020 8127 7330
sagerandwilde.com

Slick wine bar with unpretentious attitudes. Food includes heavenly cheese toasties and charcuterie.

For cocktails

19 Satan's Whiskers
343 Cambridge Heath Road E2 9RA
020 7739 8362
satanswhiskersblr.tumblr.com

Mad, darkly lit, exposed brick cocktail bar filled with skeletons and a collection of taxidermy.

For big dinner

20 Typing Room
Patriot Square E2 9NF
020 7871 0461
typingroom.com

The kitchen is headed up by Lee Westcott, who offers five- or seven-courses of his superb modern European cuisine in a stylish moss-coloured dining room with exceptionally comfy chairs.

For long coffee

21 Wilton Way Café
63 Wilton Way E8 1BG
londonfieldsradio.co.uk/the-cafe

Cute community café decked out with corrugated iron and wooden serving stations, upcycled shelving and playful lampshades. Serves locally roasted Climpson & Sons coffee.

BOOK A ROOM

For architectural finery

22 Town Hall Hotel
Patriot Square E2 9NF
020 7871 0460
townhallhotel.com

Revealing design
Subscribe now
disegnodaily.com/magazine

Disegno.
PHOTO Kevin Davies
at Jasper Morrison's
studio for Disegno No 8

SOUTHWARK & BERMONDSEY

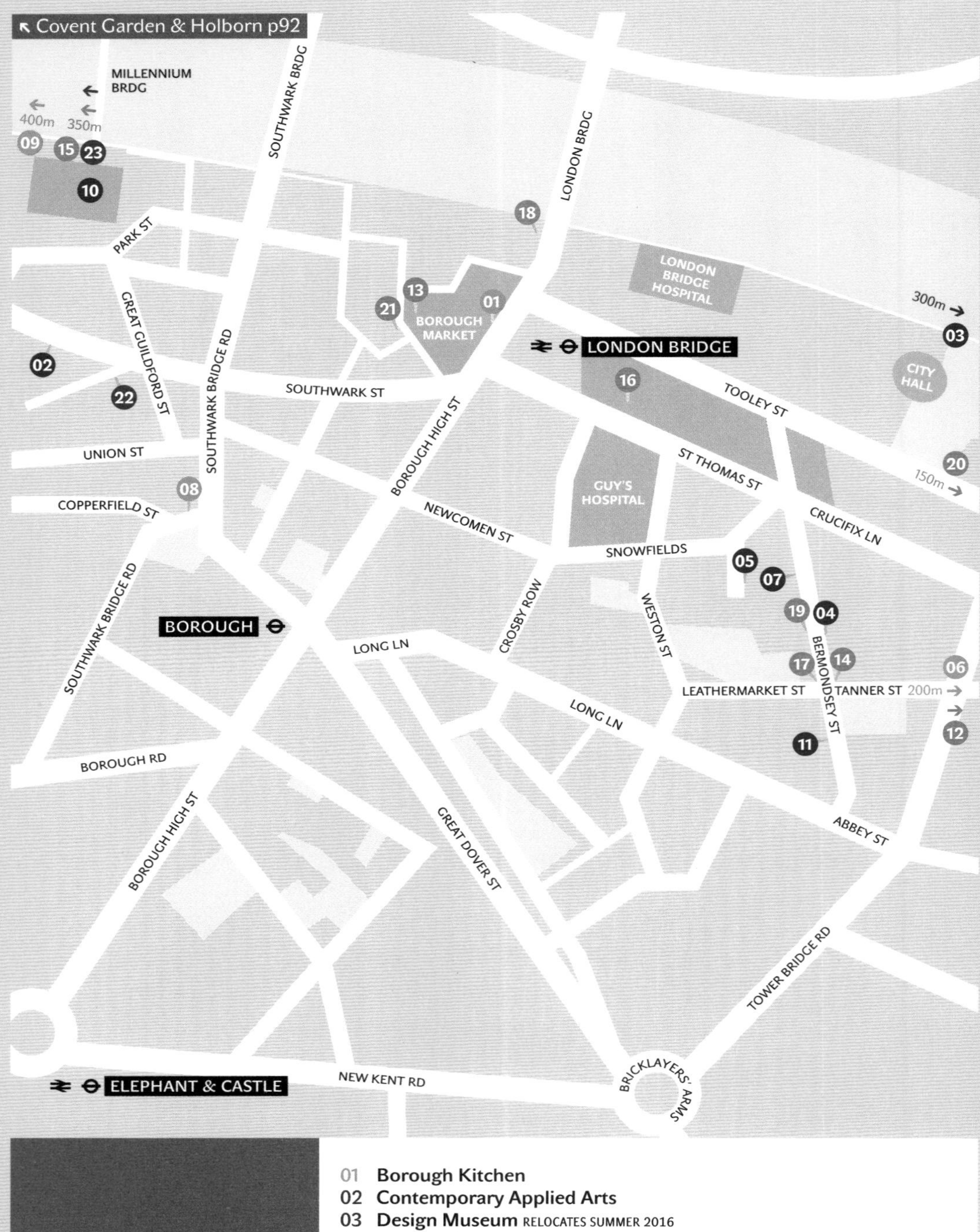

Design galleries & institutions
Design shops & C20th vintage
Design bookshops
Eat, drink & sleep (pages 192–193)

01 **Borough Kitchen**
02 **Contemporary Applied Arts**
03 **Design Museum** RELOCATES SUMMER 2016
04 **Fashion & Textile Museum**
05 **Helen Yardley Gallery**
06 **Lassco Ropewalk**
07 **London Glassblowing**
08 **Loophouse**
09 **OXO Tower Wharf**
10 **Tate Modern**
11 **White Cube Bermondsey**

Southwark & Bermondsey

The widespread appeal of Bankside and beyond has been a slow burn. Creatives have quietly toiled for decades in the crannies of Union and Bermondsey Streets, but the appearance of Tate Modern and the growth of Borough Market have had an extraordinary knock-on effect. Gradually the quarter has been repopulated by businesses and private residents, and retailers are opening to guaranteed footfall.

01 Borough Kitchen
16 Borough High Street SE1 9QG
020 3302 4260
boroughkitchen.com
Mon–Fri 10–7, Sat 9–6, Sun 12–5

In foodie paradise Borough Market sits Borough Kitchen, equipping cooks with all the tools they need. It claims to have tested everything to meet the expectations of the most rigorous of chefs, and offers up a tidy selection of everything from pots and pans, baking equipment, knives and electrical devices to serving tools and tableware.

02 Contemporary Applied Arts
89 Southwark Street SE1 0HX
020 7620 0086
caa.org.uk
Mon–Sat 10–6, Sun 11–5

This stalwart applied-arts gallery, on the ground floor of a Grade II-listed former foundry modernised by architects Allies & Morrison, launches a new show every few months, and houses an equally enriching shop.

03 Design Museum
28 Shad Thames SE1 2YD
020 7940 8790
designmuseum.org
Daily 10–5.45

In 2016, the Design Museum will inhabit the former Commonwealth Institute in Kensington, but until then, the 25-year-old institution founded by Terence Conran will remain in its art deco digs at Shad Thames. (See pages 17 and 18–23)

04 Fashion & Textile Museum
83 Bermondsey Street SE1 3XF
020 7407 8664
ftmlondon.org
Tues–Sat 11–6, Thurs 11–8, Sun 11–5

The cutting-edge institution of fuchsia-haired fashion designer Zandra Rhodes honours the giants of style with brave, brilliantly researched exhibitions on the likes of textile designer Lucienne Day and couturier Hardy Amies. The shop is worth a stop for its vitrine of vintage Barbie dolls and inventive jewellery and textiles ranges.

Art of the matter

You don't need a Guggenheim for the Bilbao effect. A tight community of galleries, small to large, is shifting London's artistic centre of gravity south of the Thames

Tate Modern, the monolithic beacon of Bankside, opened in 2000, yet for all the traffic it produced over the next few years, it could've been propped up like a film flat. Few people ever saw it from the back – there was no reason to delve that far into Southwark.

Coaxing people past Bankside's historic façades has been a struggle for galleries like Purdy Hicks, quite literally in the Tate's shadow on Hopton Street, and the 250-square-metre space at Jerwood Visual Arts, behind the railway arches on Union Street. But the residential development that began with luxury flats near the river and radiated south has brought refurbishment to crumbling urban spaces, followed by restaurants and more art and design.

"One of our big problems," says Christine Lalumia, executive director of Contemporary Applied Arts (CAA), "is that Tate Modern is such a huge magnet, people tend to come from the front or Blackfriars and don't stop in at us. We're trying to improve that by changing our signage."

CAA was lured from Fitzrovia to Southwark Street by architect firm Allies and Morrison, who wanted to lease its ground-floor storefront to "an authentic one-off," says Lalumia. "The phrase being bandied was 'not a Tesco', something that would be

Opposite, Contemporary Applied Arts

Above, White Cube Bermondsey

sympathetic to a thriving architectural practice." Some of her makers – the potters, glassblowers and weavers at the large-scale, more conceptual end – were thrilled to be in a loftier space, in what's become a proper creative hub. "Southwark is having a moment and can compete [with Mayfair and Soho] in all sorts of ways. There's a celebration of this incredible historic area that's been overlooked and has had little art and cultural investment until now."

One of the bodies writing the cheques is Better Bankside, the tax-funded non-profit organisation that cleans, paves and matchmakes local businesses for collaborations. It created the art, music and performance festival Merge, which brought Alex Chinneck's *A Pound of Flesh for 50p (Melting House)* to Southwark Street in 2014. And it paired CAA with the luxury development Neo Bankside to exhibit a flat during the 2015 London Design Festival decorated with the gallery's ceramics. Better Bankside says it has plans to spend £8million in the area over the next five years.

With the added draw of CAA and Nolias Gallery, which recently opened a third exhibition space nearby, people are nosing around to places like Loophouse, the bespoke carpet showroom

"

Galleries are like restaurants: you need a lot of good ones to pull people into an area

"

on Southwark Bridge Road. "Galleries are like restaurants," says Lalumia. "You need a lot of good ones to pull people into an area, so there's not one single outpost like an oasis in the desert."

White Cube Bermondsey created a similar effect when it opened in 2011 on Bermondsey Street, a strip of Georgian and Victorian terraces that cuts a swathe through the borough behind Shad Thames. The Fashion & Textile Museum had anchored the street for nearly a decade, yet White Cube, a former warehouse converted by architects Casper Mueller Kneer, gave the area the boost it needed. Since then, the real estate pages have touted Bermondsey as one of London's high-growth areas, with property values increasing 20 per cent over two years. The art gallery Vitrine opened its second space on Bermondsey Street in 2012. Adding to the appeal, the celebrated glass artist Peter Layton still works out of his London Glassblowing studio; Helen Yardley designs her hand-tufted rugs from A–Z Studios round the back; and Lassco, the high-end salvage centre in foodie paradise Maltby Street, is almost too crowded to navigate on market days.

As for the residents who pitched up long before the Tate's arrival, they are "fascinated" by the changes, according to Lalumia. "Our neighbours say we've added to the streetscape. They say even though they couldn't afford to shop here, they love to window shop – just knowing we're not another Tesco." **EH**

Right, London Glassblowing

Far right, Turbine Hall, Tate Modern

---

05 Helen Yardley Gallery
A–Z Studios, 3–5 Hardwidge Street SE1 3SY
020 7403 7114
helenyardley.com
Wed–Fri 11–5, or by appointment

The designer of hand-knotted and hand-tufted rugs has created a little patch of Yorkshire in industrial Bermondsey. Most of her materials hail from Yorkshire and Dorset, though her New Zealand suppliers fill the gaps. The manufacturing line is kept busy with high-spec commissions from British architects furnishing large-scale projects around the world, but local residents visit for customised versions of samples or to attend clearance sales.

06 Lassco Ropewalk
41 Maltby Street SE1 3PA
020 7394 8061
lassco.co.uk
Mon–Fri 8.30–5, Sat 9–5, Sun 11–5

The iconic salvage depot Lassco lucked out in Maltby Street, as the Saturday food market expanded around it and offered up a constant flow of young homeowners furnishing period properties. There's a sister space in Vauxhall, but this Ropewalk location offers a more gratifying shopping experience, with the requisite scrapwood, old doors and salvaged Victorian altars enhanced by buckets of door knobs and silverware to rifle through like treasure. The little

in-house café makes a lovely alternative to the barbecue smoke outside the door.

07 London Glassblowing
62–66 Bermondsey Street SE1 3UD
020 7403 2800
londonglassblowing.co.uk
Mon–Sat 10–6

One of the first 'hot glass studios' in Europe, this old block of brown brick houses artist Peter Layton's workshop and gallery. Layton, who launched the business back in 1976, puts the whole process on show, so you can trace those objets on plinths back to the molten bubbles at the end of the blowpipe.

08 Loophouse
88 Southwark Bridge Road SE1 0EX
020 7207 7619
loophouse.com
By appointment

Lorraine Statham founded Loophouse more than two decades ago to create handmade contemporary rugs. She prefers graphic, geometric patterns in saturated colours that you really have to see in situ to come to grips with. And because the standard sizes almost never make do in homes that are increasingly renovated beyond the standard floor plan, most customers opt for the bespoke service, rugs hand-tufted from 100 per cent New Zealand wool.

Holistic home
Ilse Crawford

The accepted wisdom in the hierarchy of design is that the architects are the superstars. Interior design has always been seen as something of an after-thought; a luxury that excess budget is spent on. However, Ilse Crawford has always sought to overthrow this shortsighted attitude. To Crawford, "the interior is the life of the building" and to overlook or trivialise this discipline is to compromise the atmosphere and ultimate success of a building or space. We caught up with Crawford to talk about life in London, her favourite places and her hopes for the future of the city.

Where are you from originally?
I had a Danish mother and Canadian father who met in London and made their home here. I was born in Powis Square, w11, long before it was gentrified and went to the local primary school where I learnt early on how to stick up for my 'softie' ideas in the playground.

What keeps you in London?
Although I travel quite a lot with work, I always love to come back: the true cosmopolitanism of it, the tolerance, the strength of the creative classes and, of course, the parks – which are so rare in other big cities around the world.

Where are you based now and what do you love most about the area?
I'm based in Bermondsey and I love this part of London. It was once home to prostitutes, actors, prisons, bear pits, and plague pits. It was the one place in London where you could smell both shit and strawberry jam – by that I mean the smell of the tanneries and the Hartley's Jam factory. Spa Terminus is developing slowly in a really good way with the intention of bringing food production back to the city. I love Southwark Park – it's a beauty – or to go for a drink at the Angel in Rotherhithe, sitting right on the Thames in all its murkiness. Or I head for 40 Maltby Street, one of my favourite eateries anywhere.

What is your main frustration with London?
Bit by bit, it is being handed over to the private sector and chipped away for short-term gain. Its diversity is in danger and it is driving the young, old and less well-heeled away. Of course, London was built by developers, but there were masterplans in place. Today there is a lack of an overarching, inclusive, long-term vision.

If you were Mayor of London, what would you change immediately?
Firstly, enlightened medium density housing, using proper architects, that is affordable for older and younger people. Maybe they'd be rental properties but these need to be realistic and with safe tenure. Secondly, stop the loss of our green space in the city,

whether it's sports facilities, small parks, or planting big trees in the centre (not those weeny things they call trees). Thirdly, prioritise people over cars in legislation.

Your work is described as human-centred. Where does this thinking come from?
I grew up with the Danish notion, *hygge*, that life is made up of small moments and that these matter. Then I found myself working in an industry where left-brain values dominated: measurable matters like money, time, maintenance, image, 'coolness' and marketability. The things that were never discussed were liveability, comfort, beauty, atmosphere, tactility, warmth, and wellbeing. Whether spaces made us feel grounded, good and free. In our work as a studio we start from the very beginning to embed these values in a project.

Humans are a varied species with sometimes very particular needs and desires. How do you take this into account when approaching a new brief?
We have two eyes, two ears and one mouth, and as designers we should use them in that proportion. So

SCARPA
ANDO

often the answer is there right in front of you. In my view, there is much more to be found in reality than in abstract concepts.

Your insistence on the importance of place in interiors is really refreshing – as you say, "the interior is the life of the building." Why do you think this has been ignored for so long?
For me, it is blindingly obvious that a building should be built around the lives that will be lived within it, but it has not been the priority for many reasons. Developers are rarely involved in a property once it's sold and architecture often doesn't prioritise or have the skill sets to execute the interiors in this way. For years the interior has been relegated to being 'private space'. What is interesting is that today we want to feel 'at home' in public space. Surely the goal of any building – public or private – is for it to be used over a long period and to make people happy? To make a project really good takes passion, compassion, perseverance and commitment. It's not a job, it's a vocation. **DP**

09 OXO Tower Wharf
Barge House Street SE1 9PH
020 7021 1600
coinstreet.org
Tues–Sun 11–6

This 1930s landmark, converted in the 1990s by Coin Street Community Builders, is home to some of the city's finest contemporary makers, of wildly different persuasions, including Bodo Sperlein, who create ceramics for Mulberry and Lladró, and Innermost, who make surreal light fixtures.

10 Tate Modern
Bankside SE1 9TG
020 7887 8888
tate.org.uk
Mon–Sun 10–6, Fri–Sat 10–10

The most visited modern art gallery in the world doesn't have just one superlative shop, it has four. But the ground floor space – with everything from its immense wall of books (some rare, some signed) to its divine jewellery and delicious stationery – belongs in some great museum shop hall of fame. Come early and come often: stock changes with the flavour of the exhibitions upstairs, but umpteen elbows will try to keep you from it.

11 White Cube Bermondsey
144–152 Bermondsey St SE1 3TQ
020 7930 5373
whitecube.com
Tues–Sat 10–6, Sun 12–6

At 5,000 square metres, this is not only the largest gallery in Jay Jopling's portfolio but also the largest commercial gallery in Europe. Designed by London- and Berlin-based firm Casper Mueller Kneer, the space is super-bright, super-contemporary and super-flexible, and also sports a comprehensive bookshop.

For wine and snacks
12 40 Maltby Street
40 Maltby Street SE1 3PA
020 7237 9247
40maltbystreet.com

Located in a wine warehouse on the edge of Maltby Street weekend market, this tiny brickworked bar specialises in wine from small producers and thoughtful cooking.

For Middle Eastern breakfast
13 Arabica
3 Rochester House
Borough Market SE1 9AF
020 3011 5151
arabicabarandkitchen.com

Middle Eastern restaurant with a warehouse feel. Try homemade orange and cardamom jams on toast, or delicious za'atar man'ousheh with poached eggs.

For petit lunch
14 Casse-croute
109 Bermondsey Street SE1 3XB
020 7407 2140
cassecroute.co.uk

A little piece of France in London with a menu du jour, sweet service, old Parisian prints, and red and white tablecloths.

For curious cocktails
15 Dandelyan
Mondrian at Sea Containers
20 Upper Ground SE1 9PD
020 3747 1000
morganshotelgroup.com

This hotel bar, with gold and mauve interior, bottle green velvet and leather sofas, and exquisite design by Tom Dixon, offers exciting and unusual cocktails by Ryan Chetiyawardana.

For drinks with benefits
16 Hutong
The Shard, 31 St Thomas Street SE1
020 3011 1257
hutong.co.uk

Head up to level 33 of The Shard, with amazing views across to St Paul's Cathedral, and enjoy chilli martinis, surrounded by red lanterns under a bamboo ceiling.

For pre-dinner copita
17 José
104 Bermondsey Street SE1 3UB
020 7403 4902
josepizarro.com

A busy corner bar that's great fun for several glasses of sherry and a good range of delectable Spanish cheeses and cured meats. Low ceilings and standing room tables.

For a coffee kick
18 London Grind
2 London Bridge SE1 9RA
020 7378 1928
londongrind.com

This latest branch of the slick espresso bar chain is set out in concrete and wood with neon signage. Come for the strong, smooth, house-blended coffee and squidgy banana bread.

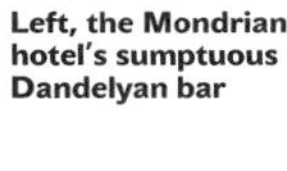

Left, the Mondrian hotel's sumptuous Dandelyan bar

Above, eye-popping interiors at pastry mecca Southerden

Eat, drink & sleep

For crafted pastries
19 Southerden Patisserie and Café
72 Bermondsey Street SE1 3UD
020 7378 1585
southerden.com

It's worth dropping by just for the eye-popping interior designed by Eley Kishimoto and Studio MacLean, but this is also a place for all of your sweet and savoury pastry desires. Look out for the salted caramel doughnuts.

For all-out dinner
20 Story
199 Tooley Street SE1 2JX
020 7183 2117
restaurantstory.co.uk

Wunderkind Tom Sellers has won a Michelin star for his sublime reinterpretations of classic British dishes. The restaurant's design sets Scandinavian minimalism against plenty of brickwork.

For lunch or dinner
21 Wright Bros Borough Market
11 Stoney Street SE1 9AD
020 7403 9554
thewrightbrothers.co.uk

Classy wooden and pea green dining room and oyster bar serving up great potted shrimp, dressed crab, and homely haddock fish pie.

BOOK A ROOM

For capsule luxury
22 CitizenM London
20 Lavington Street SE1 0NZ
020 3519 1111
citizenm.com

For riverside views
23 Mondrian London
20 Upper Ground SE1 9PD
020 3747 1000
mondrianlondon.com

CITYWIDE

BRENT
CAMDEN
ISLINGTON
HACKNEY
CITY
TOWER HAMLETS
KENSINGTON & CHELSEA
WESTMINSTER
SOUTHWARK
HAMMERSMITH & FULHAM
WANDSWORTH
LAMBETH
LEWISHAM
MERTON
CROYDON
BROMLEY
Design galleries & institutions
Design shops & C20th vintage
Design bookshops
01 52 Meters
02 Alfies Antique Market
03 Bentply
04 Case Furniture
05 Channels
06 Chaplins
07 Circus Antiques
08 Designs of Modernity
09 Do South
10 Future and Found
11 IKEA
12 Indish
13 Michael Anastassiades
14 Nook
15 Places and Spaces
16 Planet Bazaar
17 Retrouvius
18 Roca London Gallery
19 Southbank Centre Shop
20 Wellcome Collection

Citywide

London is a city of neighbourhoods, each with its own distinct character, despite doomsayers forecasting the death of the high street. What's home to one is a destination to another, and each place we feature here merits the swipe of your Oyster card. If you're familiar with the Southbank Centre, duck behind for a peek at Michael Anastassiades' window. If you're a regular at Alfies Antique Market, you'll get a kick out of its neighbour Bentply. After brunch in Stoke Newington, fit in a trip to Nook. Visit vintage paradise by way of Kensal Green. What goes for London goes for its design landscape: if you're tired of it, you're tired of life.

01 52 Meters
291 Lillie Road SW6 7LL
020 7381 1774
52meters.com
Mon-Sat 10-5.30
West Brompton tube

On a charming stretch of road crammed with antiques shops, 52 Meters is by far the most exciting, eschewing the oxidised-zinc washtubs for theatrical art deco mirrors, 1950s Italian olive-wood side tables, and school seats from Cambridge University that are more Prouvé than Prouvé.

02 Alfies Antique Market
13-25 Church Street NW8 8DT
020 7723 6066
alfiesantiques.com
Tues-Sat 10-6
Edgware Road tube

Alfies has the highest concentration of antique dealers for miles. They're knowledgeable, well connected and beloved by magazine stylists across the country. And for Murano glass devotees, Alfies is the Holy Grail. Dealers like Thirteen, Francesca Martire and Vincenzo Caffarella stock OTT lighting festooned with fanciful glass shapes.

03 Bentply
95 Lisson Grove NW1 6UP
020 7725 9515
bentply.com
Tues-Sat 11-5
Edgware Road tube

Don't be deceived by the name – there are surprisingly few bentply items on sale in this 20th century dealer's corner location on Lisson Grove, just a block away from Alfies Antique Market. Crammed into two small floors are original items of furniture, lighting and occasional accessories from 1920s–1970s. Rare 1960s brass wall lights hang above an Alvar Aalto desk; 1920s consoles sit beside four Ico Parisi dining chairs and a 1950s Olivetti table. As with any dealer, if you're looking for something particular, call in advance of a visit or ask on arrival.

04 Case Furniture
23 East Hill SW18 2HZ
020 8870 4488
casefurniture.co.uk
Mon–Fri 10–6, Sat 10–4
Wandsworth Town rail

Case does an essential job in filling a gap in the market that too often gets hijacked by mediocrity. Stocking furniture by the likes of Bill Amberg, Shin Azumi, Marina Bautier, Robin Day, Matthew Hilton, Nazamin Kamali, Hierve and Samuel Wilkinson, this place hits the mark for those looking for top quality design that doesn't break the bank.

05 Channels
1–3 New Kings Road SW6 4SB
020 7371 0301
channelsdesign.com
Mon–Sat 10–5.30
Fulham Broadway tube

A supreme calm reigns in Samuel Chan's studio. There's wood everywhere, tactile and satin smooth, begging to be stroked. Chan works in oak, walnut, reclaimed cedar, or whatever his bespoke clients want. There's a Nordic/Asian vibe, with armchairs borrowing heavily from Wegner but adding scrolled armrests that wouldn't look out of place in the Forbidden City in the 1920s.

06 Chaplins
477–507 Uxbridge Road, Hatch End, Middlesex HA5 4JS
020 8421 1779
chaplins.co.uk
Mon–Sat 10–6
Hatch End rail

London's largest retailer of high-end furniture, lighting and interior products lies on the northwest fringes of the city. Its enormous showroom features top quality pieces produced by the likes of Vitra, Moroso, B&B Italia, Moooi, Ligne Roset, Molteni&C, Cassina, Arper, Magis and more. Items are given space to breathe in carefully styled room sets, and staff are on hand to inform and advise.

07 Circus Antiques
60 Chamberlayne Road NW10 3JH
020 8968 8244
circusantiques.co.uk
Tues–Fri 10.30–5.30, Sat 10.30–5
Kensal Green tube/Kensal Rise rail

This packed showroom has all the excitement of a junk shop without any junk. There's furniture and lighting dating back as far as the 19th century right up to the mid-20th century, mostly from France and Italy. You may find some familiar names here, but the vintage stock has been chosen for its visual appeal as much as its pedigree. Lighting is a particularly strong suit – everything from 1950s Italian chandeliers to colossal theatre lights – and there's always a good selection of mirrors and coffee tables.

08 Designs of Modernity
Crystal Palace Antiques, Jasper Road SE19 1SG
07966 285 694
designsofmodernity.com
Mon–Sat 10–6, Sun 10–5
Crystal Palace tube

You're likely to see some iconic pieces at this fine purveyor of midcentury style, but the real treasures are less familiar – a sideboard by John and Sylvia Reid, a Fog & Morup lamp or a funky poster from the Munich Olympics. The furniture and lighting, sourced on regular trips to the Netherlands, Antwerp and Stockholm, is of a consistently high quality with a particular bias towards combining metal with lots of beautiful teak. A regularly updated website can keep you in the loop, but if you're able to visit in person, do. Browsing here is a delight.

09 Do South
2 Westow Street SE19 3AH
020 8771 0500
dosouthshop.com
Mon–Fri 11–6, Sat 10–6, Sun 11–5
Crystal Palace tube

Occupying a prime corner spot with breathtaking views across London, this vintage and

Above, top quality design at Case Furniture, Wandsworth

DIFFUSEUR DE PARFUM EXTRA PUR FIGUE
BOUGIE PARFUMÉE EXTRA PUR FIGUE

contemporary furniture shop was established in 2011 with the aim of saving design-loving locals from having to trek into town. The best bits of the contemporary collection are clean-lined yet comfortable sofas and there are some sleek sideboards too, if you're not a fan of the midcentury variety.

10 Future and Found

225A Brecknock Road N19 5AA
020 7267 4772
futureandfound.com
Tues-Fri 10-6:30, Sat 10-6, Sun 12-6
Tufnell Park tube

Future and Found was opened by Andrea Bates in a converted piano factory in 2014, down a small alley only a stone's throw from Tufnell Park tube and the busy traffic junction. Bates' love of clean-lined, modern and geometric graphics is clear in the products she has sourced, be it chairs, shelving and lights or smaller tabletop items, cushions, stationery and gifts. While various tasteful shades of grey might sit next to textured wood grain or rich marble, a healthy injection of fluorescent adds zingy accents for a touch of colour. If you're after some addition for your home or a gift, this is the sort of secret neighbourhood store of which you'll be grateful to know about.

11 IKEA

Croydon, Edmonton & Wembley
ikea.com/gb
See website for transport details

The key to a successful IKEA experience is discipline. Plan ahead, go early and don't get distracted. If you follow the rules, you'll still leave with more than you came for, but IKEA is ideal for the dining table you can't yet afford to commission, or the wardrobe that'll keep things off the floor in your new flat. The kitchenware is as good as any; ditto the kitchen cabinets and hardware. What you don't want is to 'over IKEA'. It's easy to do, but it'll make your home bland and cookie-cutter.

12 Indish

16 Broadway Parade N8 9DE
020 8340 1188
indish.co.uk
Mon-Sat 10.30-5.30, Sun 12.30-4.30
Crouch Hill rail

Lying in the shadow of the Crouch End clock tower, in one of the area's typical redbrick shop arcades, Indish has been an essential part of life in this genteel north London enclave for more than 15 years. There's a clear Nordic bent in the selection of stock, with names reading like a who's who in Scandinavian accessible design: Normann Copenhagen, Tonfisk, Design House Stockholm, Eva Solo, Marimekko and Stelton, with a substantial sprinkling of Alessi, Donna Wilson and Orla Kiely.

13 Michael Anastassiades

122 Lower Marsh SE1 7AE
020 7928 7527
michaelanastassiades.com
Open by appointment only
Waterloo tube

Behind Waterloo station lurks Lower Marsh, an untouched slice of London at its local best. Since designer Michael Anastassiades bought his live/work space here nearly 20 years ago, the area has changed as much as the house, now curated with soaring glass walls and bespoke storage. Downstairs is the gallery, and a studio where Anastassiades and his team work on his mobile pendant lights and tableware. Guests have the opportunity to see his designs from the literal drawing board – as real as the larger-than-life London street outside. (See pages 202–203)

14 Nook

153 Stoke Newington Church Street
N16 0UH
020 7249 9436
nookshop.co.uk
Mon-Sat 10-6, Sun 11-6
Stoke Newington rail

Despite the failure of the railing residents to block the arrival of Nando's, Stoke Newington

Clean-lined chic at Future and Found in Tufnell Park

Balancing act
Michael Anastassiades

Designer Michael Anastassiades has sculpted himself an enviable set-up. He had the foresight to buy his centrally-located property on Lower Marsh – directly behind Waterloo station – when the area was neglected. He undertook a major renovation and created a tranquil haven amid a bustling neighbourhood. The building is his home as well as his design studio and shop – a perfectly curated showcase for his expanding collection of exquisite and timeless lighting, products and furniture.

You moved from Cyprus to London. What was it that attracted you to London?
I grew up in Cyprus and went to school there. There was no university at the time and anyone that wanted to pursue further studies had to go abroad. I had a British education, so coming to the UK and especially London was a great option.

When did you move to Lower Marsh and what attracted you to this street and area?
I bought my place 18 years ago. It was the only part of central London that was forgotten. I remember walking home at the time from the West End and passing through the 'cardboard city' (ad hoc shelter for the homeless). It has changed a lot since.

You converted the entire building. How have you used the space?
I gutted the whole interior of the building. I just kept the boundary walls, removed the roof and excavated deeper to create a liveable basement space. Everything inside is new, though it feels like it has always been like this. It took me 18 years to get it to where it is. I guess it will always remain an ongoing project. It is a live/work space with the studio and shop on the ground floor. Clients come and visit and can often get to view the rest of the building and see the work in context.

Your design studio is here. What sort of projects do you work on?
I constantly develop new products for my own lighting brand. I also design for various companies like Flos, Puiforcat, Svenskt Tenn and Herman Miller.

What adjectives would you use to describe your work?
Disciplined, distilled, thought provoking, layered, and humorous.

What are some of the challenges that you face operating in London?
Space is precious in London. Other than that, it is a great place to operate from and remains very inspiring. **MF**

13 **Michael Anastassiades** 122 Lower Marsh SE1 7AE
(See page 201 for full details)

Church Street is one of London's loveliest truly independent high streets. If it's not boasting a New York-style greengrocer or copper kitchenware shop, there's a trendy salon or French children's boutique taking up residence. And there's also Nook, which was launched in 2012 by longtime retailers Jack and Kate Simpson along with Jack's partner Gemma Ridgway. Nook flies the flag for smart, well-made design in the same way as Shoreditch purveyors Labour and Wait and Goodhood. The window is decorated sparsely with small jointed-wood mannequins or, on other days, dainty pieces of Falcon Enamelware. That's the hint that inside you might find the coveted Penguin Donkey bookcase, or a cast-iron pestle and mortar by Robert Welch. Local purists tsk-tsk that a Super Kim can opener from France is the last thing they need, then squeeze their buggies into the place on weekends to pick up Mast Brothers chocolate for a hostess gift or a copy of *Wrap* magazine for the office. We can't blame them: it is snug as a nook inside, a pleasant spot to stock up on Paul Farrell stationery and promise ourselves we'll use it.

15 Places and Spaces
30 Old Town SW4 0LB
020 7498 0998
placesandspaces.com
Tues-Sat 10-5.45, Sun 12-4
Clapham Common tube

Places and Spaces caters for Clapham Common's Stokke-toting parents. There's a clear predilection for wooden toys, with games from Brio and Kaj Bojesen's monkey swinging from the shelves, but also Asplund sideboards, Muuto coffee tables and Jieldé floor lamps for the grown-ups' delectation. The Scandinavians are heavily represented, with the now ubiquitous Moomin cups from iittala lovingly displayed and Form Us With Love's industrial lamp for Design House Stockholm shedding a gentle light on the tasteful, grey walls.

16 Planet Bazaar
Arch 68, Stables Market,
Chalk Farm Road NW1 8AH
020 7485 6000
planetbazaar.co.uk
Tues-Fri 12-5, Sat-Sun 10-5.30
Chalk Farm tube

Maureen Silverman has been trading in mementos from the 1950s through to the 1980s since 1997. This is no jumble sale though: prices are affordable yet not rock bottom (it's fodder for the Primrose Hill set, after all) and there are always gems, such as Italian modern table lamps, a surfeit of Jacobsen and Eames, and all the Chippy Heath telephone tables a flat can accommodate.

17 Retrouvius
1016 Harrow Road NW10 5NS
020 8960 6060
retrouvius.com
Mon-Sat 10-6
Kensal Green tube

Directors Adam Hills and Maria Speake have chiseled a whole new aesthetic out of found objects, a style often described in the press as 'rough luxe', 'British eclectic' or even the dreaded 'shabby chic'. But seeing all the salvaged items (lampshades, rugs, benches, signs) in situ, in the cavernous warehouse, they take on a whole new life, breathing beauty in a way they probably never did fresh from the workshop. It's a design style much emulated but rarely bettered.

18 Roca London Gallery
Station Court, Townmead Road
SW6 2PY
020 7610 9503
rocalondongallery.com
Mon-Fri 9-5.30, Sat 11-5
Imperial Wharf tube

Designed by the great dame of pioneering architecture Zaha Hadid, this is possibly the most striking and futuristic bathroom showroom you are ever likely to find. At a base level, this is a 1,100-square-metre showroom for Spanish brand Roca to display

Right, the Zaha Hadid-designed Roca London Gallery

its ranges of taps, basins, toilets, showers and baths. But it also hosts an array of exhibitions and talks that draw attention to the global importance of water for humanity, offering enterprising solutions to water shortage, pollution and distribution.

19 Southbank Centre Shop
Festival Terrace SE1 8XX
020 7921 0771
shop.southbankcentre.co.uk
Mon-Fri 10-9, Sat 10-8, Sun 12-8
Waterloo tube

Whether it's a conscious effort or not by buyer Katherine Walsh, this shop mirrors the ethos of inclusiveness that was the basis of the Festival of Britain back in 1951, making design and art accessible to all without conceding on quality and vision. In the choice of products there are also discernible ties backwards, with Mini Modern's wallpaper harking back to a midcentury aesthetic, but this is weighed up by an equally strong forward vision, as seen in the Flux chairs, made from one foldable sheet of polypropylene.

20 Wellcome Collection
183 Euston Road NW1 2BE
020 7611 2222
wellcomecollection.org
Tues-Sat 10-6, Thurs 10-10, Sun 11-6
Euston Square tube/Euston rail

This rare treasure manages to make even medicine sexy. Located in a 1932 neoclassical pile, it houses an exciting collection of medical curiosities (from Japanese sex toys to Napoleon's toothbrush). A series of bright spaces upstairs hosts the permanent collection, wired with nifty technology that encourages interaction. Skeletons are curiously jumbled; a transparent body has organs that light up when you push their buttons; and supersized minibeasts appear in vitrines. It also puts on a schedule of out-there exhibitions highlighting the confluence of life, death, discovery, art and design.

Index

Credits

British Library Cataloguing-in-Publication data. A catalogue record for this book is available from the British Library.

Although the authors, editors, and publisher made every effort to ensure that the information contained in this publication is up-to-date and as accurate as possible at the time of going to press, some details are liable to change. The publisher accepts no responsibility for any loss, injury, damage or inconvenience sustained to any person using this book.

Printed in The Netherlands by Wilco Printing & Binding

MIX
Paper from responsible sources
FSC® C004472

G . F SMITH
1885 ONWARDS

This guide is printed on G.F Smith paper, the cover on 400gsm and the text on 120gsm Naturalis Absolute White Smooth.

Publisher's acknowledgements: Spotlight Press would like to thank all contributing shops, galleries, institutions, designers, agencies and photographers for their kind permissions to reproduce their images in this book.

Photography credits: all photography credited to Jessica Klingelfuss, apart from pages: 18, 19 & 22 Andrew + Tye; 21 Alex Morris; 29 Bulgari Hotel & Residences London; 47 The Laslett; 56 Paul Raeside; 66 Edition Hotels; 67 Patricia Niven; 69 John Carey; p82 Stuart Keegan; 84 Julian Abrams; 86 Xavier Girard Lachaîne; 88 Carol Sachs (Bao), Ed Reeve (Hoi Polloi), Yuki Sugiura (The Clove Club), POLPO; 89 The Mandarin Oriental London (Dinner by Heston Blumenthal), Ed Reeve (Blixen); 102 Barrafina; 103 Amber Rowlands; 120 Mark Cocksedge (bottom); 122 Anya Holdstock; 123 John Carey; 133 Ming Tang-Evans; 157 Ed Reeve (top), Patricia Niven (bottom); 158 Rosewood London; 160 Edition Hotels, Andrew Meredith (Ace Hotel London Shoreditch); 161 Rosewood London, CitizenM; 166 John Short; 176 Joe Woodhouse; 177 John Carey; 185 Tate Photography; 186–191 Leslie Williamson; 192 Niall Clutton.